EASY LOW-CAL VEGAN EATS

60 Flavor-Packed Recipes with Less Than
400 CALORIES PER SERVING

JILLIAN GLENN, Creator of Peanut Butter and Jilly

First published in 2021 by

Page Street Publishing Co.

27 Congress Street, Suite 105

Salem, MA 01970

www.pagestreetpublishing.com

Distributed by Macmillan, sales in Canada by The Canadian Manda Group.

25 24 23 22 21 1 2 3 4 5

ISBN-13: 978-1-64567-326-2

ISBN-10: 1-64567-326-X

Library of Congress Control Number: 2020948565

Cover and book design by Laura Benton for Page Street Publishing Co.

Photography by Somer Handley and Jillian Glenn

Props and staging by Maureen Onda

Printed and bound in China

Page Street Publishing protects our planet by donating to nonprofits like The Trustees, which focuses on local land conservation.

To those who are seeking flavorful, healthy, balanced, plant-based meals for yourself and your family.

To those who are searching for easier and lighter ways to enjoy delicious and nutritious food without animal by-products.

To those who have decided to try a plant-based diet due to health reasons, compassion for animals, our ecosystem or any other reason.

To the followers and readers of Peanut Butter and Jilly, who allow me to be a little part of their lives each day and make what I do so fun.

To my family and friends, who are my greatest recipe testers, cheerleaders and my heart and soul.

To God, for without You, none of this would have been possible.

CONTENTS

NUTRITIOUS & NEVER BORING DINNERS 63

SAVORY SOUPS & PLANT-PROTEIN SALADS 103

THERE'S ALWAYS ROOM FOR DESSERT 119

INTRODUCTION

Hi there! My name is Jill and I create easy, low-calorie and balanced vegan and gluten-free recipes that are simple, craveable and family-friendly. I love food, and I care as much about flavor as I do about nutrition. I also have a killer sweet tooth, so along with a whole-foods diet, I eat dessert every day—and you can, too!

I started following a plant-based diet after learning about how high meat and dairy consumption is linked with many chronic illnesses. Before going plant based, I struggled with digestive issues, such as lactose intolerance, and always felt sluggish after eating meat. My energy levels used to bounce up and down, and so did my weight. Now, my energy levels are higher than ever, my digestive issues have virtually disappeared, I'm no longer afraid of carbs and I've managed to maintain my weight easily. I don't ever see myself eating meat or dairy again. Why? I never feel that I'm missing out on delicious foods! In fact, I enjoy more of my favorite foods now than I ever did before. And, I have discovered many new and exciting ways to incorporate flavor and healthier ingredients.

When I first started following a plant-based diet, my friends and family had their doubts. I took this as a challenge and began to prepare my tasty vegan dishes for them. Things like my famous Super-Moist Lemon Loaf (page 135), vegan donuts, Streusel-Topped Oatmeal Coffee Cake (page 23), pastas, pizzas and burrito bowls. Everyone started calling, asking for my recipes and how I managed to eat all of this comfort food while staying lean and fit. That's how my blog, Peanut Butter and Jilly, was born. Today, Peanut Butter and Jilly has hundreds of thousands of readers who follow my low-calorie and delicious vegan recipes. Most of my dishes are also gluten free or can be made gluten free with simple swaps.

After sharing my recipes online, my readers started asking for a cookbook. Many of them wanted to know more about my food philosophy and how I eat what I love and maintain my shape. I decided to write this book so that they too could enjoy the yummy foods they love in a lighter, plant-based, healthy(ish) way. I am certified in nutrition and truly believe that part of enjoying a healthy and balanced diet is never depriving yourself. Which is why I always save room for a little indulgence! Treating myself to something slightly sugary is what keeps me motivated and on track throughout the day. For you, it might be something savory instead. Whatever it is, this cookbook has recipes to help you satisfy that hankering while staying on track with your plant-based diet and health goals.

The recipes you will find here include yummy breakfast favorites, including Warm Apple Cinnamon Oatmeal Pancakes (page 12) and Unbelievably Vegan Cinnamon Rolls (page 15). You will discover tasty, lean lunches, such as the Mediterranean Power Bowl (page 41), healthy loaded baked potato recipes and Tasty Fajita Veggie Wraps (page 46). When you're ready to enjoy your evening meal, there's a plethora of quick sheet-pan dinners, such as Baked Black Bean Burgers with Avocado Salsa (page 67), Creamy Lemon Garlic Pasta (page 100), mouthwatering stir-fry meals, fried rice and vegan pizzas to choose from. If you're in the mood for a comforting soup or a satisfying and protein-packed salad, I've got you covered! And the day isn't complete without dessert. Choose from scrumptious favorites such as Snickerdoodle Cookies (page 120), Mama's Maple Butter Crescent Rolls (page 123), Healthy Oatmeal Carrot Cake (page 139) and more. The best part is that every single one of the recipes in this book is low calorie but will leave you feeling full and super satisfied.

There are ways to enjoy the foods you love while feeling and looking great. Whether you're 100-percent vegan or just looking to incorporate more plant-based meals into your diet, my goal is to help you serve yourself and others balanced dishes that taste amazing. And, seriously, don't skip dessert. Life's too short!

Before we get started in the kitchen, I'd like to share a bit more about my food philosophy and tips to enjoying your light, lean and tasty lifestyle.

EAT IN MORE

I love a home-cooked meal and I will take an evening in preparing a delicious dinner over going out to eat any day. When I have guests, I look forward to waking them up with the heavenly aroma of homemade cinnamon rolls or oatmeal banana bread. It's always fun to feed non-vegans and watch as they delight in one of their first plant-based meals! When you prepare your own meals, you know exactly what you're consuming, which helps you manage your calories and make healthier choices. It gives you more control over your food and how it's prepared. This allows you to enjoy the food you love in a lighter way (baking, not frying; less oil; almond milk versus cow's milk; etc.).

PLAN AHEAD

For anyone seeking a healthier diet, planning ahead is key. Which is why you will find plenty of make-ahead meals to help keep you on track. For example, if you're in a scramble in the morning and running out the door, you might be tempted to grab a highly processed and sugary toaster pastry. But, if you had taken five to ten minutes the night before to whip up a blueberry baked oatmeal and throw it in the oven while you continued on with your evening to-dos, you would have had a delicious and healthy breakfast to reheat and enjoy. Not only will the second option taste better, but the protein, complex carbohydrates, fruit and healthy fats will sustain you longer, making you less likely to crash and overeat later.

CHOOSE MORE VOLUME FOODS

These are foods that take up a lot of space in your tummy for a low number of calories. These foods are typically high in fiber and usually nutritious! When my stomach feels full and my body is receiving the nutrients it needs, I'm less likely to consume unnecessary calories. My favorite volume foods include oatmeal, cauliflower, berries and other fruits, virtually any vegetable, spaghetti squash and other gourds as well as legumes. I try to incorporate at least one of these foods into almost all of my meals.

HAVE NO FOOD REMORSE

I know so many people who suffer from "food guilt." Food guilt happens to me whenever I overindulge in something unhealthy. I've found a way to never experience food remorse again and my secret is to simply enjoy clean, light and healthy foods 90 percent of the time, and build in a 10 percent splurge so I don't feel deprived. For me, that's a snickerdoodle cookie. For you, it might be a slice of my tasty vegan pizza! Which brings me to my next point.

NEVER DEPRIVE YOURSELF

Instead, make good healthful and balanced choices. Save your calories for the good stuff that you love. For instance, I'd rather enjoy a protein-packed salad instead of French fries. By doing this, I'm saving myself a few hundred calories and choosing a nutritious dish that will keep me satisfied longer without weighing me down. Now, I have room for delicious and healthier homemade banana cookies later! And, I don't feel guilty about the cookies because I didn't eat them impulsively—I planned for them and fit them into my calorie allotment. Figure out the foods you love to eat, enjoy them in the healthiest way and keep it clean the rest of the time!

COUNT CALORIES

I've been able to manage my weight easily and without sacrificing the foods I love by using simple math: "Calories In versus Calories Out." Which is why I've included calorie counts for all the recipes in this book. The quality of your calories matters, too. Eating a balanced amount of plant protein, healthy plant-based fats, complex carbohydrates, legumes, nuts, seeds and tons of fruits and veggies will help you feel and look your best.

Everyone's body is unique and special and your diet is just one component of living a healthy lifestyle. I have a holistic approach to wellness and believe in getting consistent exercise, quality sleep, staying well hydrated and taking time for self-love. I encourage myself and others to make the healthier choice at each meal while also always allowing room for mindful and non-impulsive indulgences. Nothing in this book replaces a doctor's recommendation.

BREAKFAST:

THE MOST DELICIOUS MEAL OF THE DAY

Many people believe that breakfast is the most important meal of the day. In my opinion, it's also the most delicious! I like my breakfast how I like all of my meals: plant based, healthy(ish), filling and super tasty. If you're a breakfast person like me, you're going to love this chapter. Whether it's sinking your teeth into a stack of Warm Apple Cinnamon Oatmeal Pancakes (page 12), smearing vegan cream cheese on the On-the-Run Everything Bagel Bites (page 19) or buttering a warm slice of Fluffy Oatmeal Banana Bread (page 16), these yummy low-calorie vegan breakfasts are sure to please your palate.

Within this chapter, you will find weekday options, such as Grab & Go Oatmeal Raisin Granola Bars (page 35) or Nutritious Blueberry Baked Oatmeal (page 24), as well as weekend favorites like Unbelievably Vegan Cinnamon Rolls (page 15) or Streusel-Topped Oatmeal Coffee Cake (page 23). Every scrumptious recipe clocks in under 400 calories, can be made gluten free, packs in the flavor and will keep you full until lunch. Here are some inviting vegan dishes that will cause you to actually look forward to waking up in the morning!

WARM APPLE CINNAMON OATMEAL PANCAKES

YIELD: 5 SERVINGS
(4 PANCAKES WITH 1 TBSP [15 ML] OF MAPLE SYRUP)
CALORIES: 294 PER SERVING

For those who love waking up to a golden stack of pancakes that are crisp on the outside and soft on the inside, this recipe is for you! These pancakes are full of oats and delicious apples and cinnamon. Oats are one of my favorite ways to incorporate more fiber and texture into pancakes and other sweet dishes. It always makes foods more filling and satisfying! Drizzle your pancakes with warm maple syrup and serve them with apple slices for a healthy and balanced vegan breakfast that you'll want to devour.

2 cups (480 ml) unsweetened almond milk

1 cup (240 ml) unsweetened applesauce

2 tbsp (30 ml) pure maple syrup, plus more for serving

2 tsp (9 g) baking powder

1 tsp ground cinnamon

1 tsp vanilla extract

1½ cups (135 g) quick oats

1 cup (125 g) regular or gluten-free all-purpose flour (I prefer King Arthur Gluten-Free Measure for Measure Flour)

Nonstick spray, for pan

Apple slices, for serving (optional)

In a large bowl, whisk together the almond milk, applesauce, maple syrup, baking powder, cinnamon and vanilla. Mix in the quick oats and flour until a batter forms.

Heat a medium-sized skillet over medium-low heat. Spray it with nonstick spray. Once the skillet is hot, spoon in about 2 tablespoons (30 ml) of batter per pancake. Cook for about 5 minutes, or until bubbles begin to form on the top of the pancake. Use a spatula to flip. The cooked side should be golden brown. Cook for another 3 to 5 minutes on the other side. Use your spatula to gently lift the pancake off the skillet to check whether it's golden on the bottom side yet. Repeat until all the batter is used. This recipe makes about 20 pancakes.

Drizzle with more maple syrup and top with apple slices, if desired.

UNBELIEVABLY VEGAN CINNAMON ROLLS

YIELD: 10 CINNAMON ROLLS
CALORIES: 323 PER CINNAMON ROLL

If you are looking for a delicious vegan breakfast to impress your guests, go for a batch of these. The heavenly aroma of baking homemade dough wrapped around buttery cinnamon-sugar filling will make everyone's mouth water. And, once you drizzle them with the addictive icing, your family will be fighting over the last bite. Oh, and they definitely won't believe these are vegan.

---

1 cup (240 ml) unsweetened almond milk

¼ cup (60 ml) melted vegan butter

2 tbsp (30 ml) pure maple syrup

½ tsp salt

2 tsp (10 g) baking powder (only use if baking with gluten-free flour)

1 tbsp (12 g) active dry yeast

1 tbsp (15 ml) apple cider vinegar (only use if baking with gluten-free flour)

2½ cups (300 g) regular or gluten-free all-purpose flour (I prefer King Arthur Gluten-Free Measure for Measure Flour), plus more for rolling

½ cup (114 g) softened vegan butter, divided

½ cup (100 g) cane sugar

2 tsp (5 g) ground cinnamon

4 oz (114 g) vegan cream cheese

1½ cups (180 g) confectioners' sugar

In a microwave-safe bowl, microwave the almond milk for about 45 seconds so it's warm, but not hot. Pour it into a large bowl and stir in the melted vegan butter, maple syrup and salt. If you're using gluten-free flour, add the baking powder and mix. Sprinkle the yeast evenly over the top of the mixture, gently stir two or three times and allow it to sit for about 10 minutes. After 10 minutes, if you're using gluten-free flour, add the apple cider vinegar and mix. If not, proceed to the next step.

Add the flour and mix until a thick dough forms. Stop mixing once a dough forms to avoid overmixing. Use your hands to gently form the dough into a round mound. Leave the dough in the bowl and cover the bowl with a clean kitchen towel. Allow it to rise for 1 to 2 hours. I like to set the bowl of dough on top of a preheated 350°F (175°C) oven. The warmth of the oven helps the dough rise faster.

Once the dough has doubled in size (Note: if using gluten-free all-purpose flour, the dough will rise less), lay it on a floured surface and roll it into a ⅓-inch (8-mm)-thick rectangle. You may need to sprinkle a little flour on top if the dough is too sticky to roll.

Spread ¼ cup (57 g) of the softened vegan butter on the rolled dough, then sprinkle with the cane sugar and cinnamon. Use your hands to roll the dough into a log, then slice it into ten pinwheels. Place the pinwheels into a standard casserole dish or round baking dish. Make sure there is room in the dish for the rolls to almost double in size. Cover the dish with a clean towel, set it aside and allow the dough to rise for another 30 minutes. You can set it on top of the warm oven again.

If you haven't done so already, preheat the oven to 350°F (175°C). Remove the towel from the rolls and bake them for 30 to 35 minutes, or until golden and fluffy.

Meanwhile, in a bowl, combine the vegan cream cheese, remaining ¼ cup (57 g) of softened vegan butter and confectioners' sugar and use an electric hand mixer to mix them together. Set aside or store in the fridge until ready to serve. Once the rolls are done baking, remove them from the oven and wait for 5 to 10 minutes for them to cool before spreading about half of the icing over the rolls. Serve warm with additional icing on the side.

If you have leftover icing, you may store it in the fridge for 2 to 3 days or in the freezer for up to a month.

FLUFFY OATMEAL BANANA BREAD

YIELD: 10 SLICES
CALORIES: 195 CALORIES PER SLICE

Whenever a fresh loaf of this tender and moist banana bread comes out of the oven, no one can resist having a slice! This fluffy loaf makes the perfect breakfast, but it's also great any time of day! It's an awesome way to use up your overripe bananas. I personally think that vegan banana bread is better than non-vegan banana bread. At least . . . this one is. It's moist, soft and delicious, and the oats in the batter will keep you feeling full all morning. While banana bread is totally worth indulging in, the nice thing about this recipe is that you don't have to! At under 200 calories a serving, you can enjoy a warm slice or two without worry.

Nonstick cooking spray, for pan

3 medium-sized mashed ripe bananas

1 cup (240 ml) unsweetened almond milk

¾ cup (180 ml) pure maple syrup

4 tbsp (60 ml) melted vegan butter

1 tsp vanilla extract

1 tsp ground cinnamon

1 tsp baking soda

2 tsp (9 g) baking powder

1½ cups (180 g) regular or gluten-free all-purpose flour (I prefer King Arthur Gluten-Free Measure for Measure Flour)

1 cup (90 g) quick oats, plus a few for sprinkling

Preheat the oven to 375°F (190°C). Spray a 9 x 5-inch (23 x 13-cm) loaf pan with nonstick cooking spray.

In a large bowl, mash the bananas with a fork, then mix in the almond milk, maple syrup, melted vegan butter, vanilla, cinnamon, baking soda and baking powder until combined. Using your fork, stir in the flour and quick oats. Mix the batter until combined and pour it into the prepared loaf pan. Sprinkle the top of the loaf with a few oats for decor. Definitely lick the spoon!

Bake the loaf for 40 to 45 minutes (times may vary based on the material of your loaf pan). When the loaf is done, it will be golden on top and you should be able to stick a toothpick into the center of it without batter on the withdrawn toothpick.

Enjoy the banana bread warm or store it on the countertop in an airtight container for 2 to 3 days. It tastes great on its own, spread with vegan butter or drizzled with maple syrup.

ON-THE-RUN EVERYTHING BAGEL BITES

YIELD: 16 TO 18 BAGEL BITES
CALORIES: 193 PER 4 BITES

If I had to choose one bagel flavor to eat for the rest of my life, without a doubt, I'd choose everything bagels. I love the savory flavors of everything seasoning sprinkled over a chewy and warm bagel. Store-bought and bakery bagels can be high in calories. And traditional homemade bagels can take forever to make. Skip the yeast, boiling and rolling with these bagel bites! You can enjoy four of them for a fraction of a typical bagel's calories—which means you have more room to smear on your favorite vegan cream cheese or butter. This recipe is simple, quick and easy. Enjoy them freshly baked or bake and freeze them to pop into a toaster oven later.

Nonstick spray

2 tbsp (16 g) flaxseed meal

¼ cup (60 ml) warm water

½ cup (120 ml) unsweetened almond milk

2 tbsp (30 ml) olive oil

2 tsp (9 g) baking powder

½ tsp salt

1 cup (125 g) regular or gluten-free all-purpose flour (I prefer King Arthur Gluten-Free Measure for Measure Flour)

1 tbsp (1 g) chopped fresh chives

¼ cup (40 g) everything bagel seasoning

Vegan butter or cream cheese, for serving

Preheat the oven to 400°F (200°C). Spray 16 to 18 mini donut hole or muffin molds with nonstick spray.

Prepare your flax eggs: In a small bowl, mix the flaxseed meal with the warm water and set aside to rest for 2 minutes.

In a large bowl, mix together the almond milk, olive oil, baking powder and salt. Then, add the flax eggs while still warm and mix well. Add the flour and mix just until a dough forms and the batter is completely combined. Be careful not to work the batter too much, or the bagels will be hard. Fold in the chives and spoon the batter into the prepared molds. Sprinkle everything seasoning over the top of each bagel (about ½ teaspoon per bagel).

Bake the bagel bites for 10 to 12 minutes, or until the bites have risen and are lightly golden. Remove them from the oven and serve immediately with your favorite vegan butter or cream cheese.

You may store these on the countertop or in the freezer in an airtight container and toast them when you're ready to enjoy.

CRAVIN' CORNBREAD MUFFINS WITH BLUEBERRY BUTTER

YIELD: 14 MUFFINS
CALORIES: 169 PER MUFFIN WITH BLUEBERRY BUTTER

Here in the South, we love crumbly, slightly sweet and fluffy cornbread! The perfect cornbread is golden on the outside, soft and moist on the inside and best served warm. Many people only ever have cornbread around the holidays, but you can enjoy these comforting, delightful muffins anytime. My advice: Have them for breakfast with homemade blueberry butter! Your taste buds will experience true magic when you bite into one of these scrumptious vegan muffins spread with blueberry butter.

Baking spray (optional)

1½ cups (360 ml) canned full-fat coconut milk

½ cup (120 ml) pure maple syrup

2 tbsp (30 ml) melted coconut oil

1 tbsp (14 g) baking powder

1 cup (120 g) cornmeal

1¼ cups (156 g) regular or gluten-free all-purpose flour (I prefer King Arthur Gluten-Free Measure for Measure Flour)

1 cup (148 g) frozen wild blueberries, thawed

¼ cup (57 g) softened vegan butter

1 tbsp (8 g) confectioners' sugar

Preheat the oven to 375°F (190°C). Spray 14 muffin molds with baking spray or line with paper liners.

In a large bowl, mix together the coconut milk, maple syrup, melted coconut oil and baking powder. Then, add the cornmeal and flour and mix just until combined.

Pour the batter into the prepared muffin molds.

Bake for 30 to 35 minutes, or until risen and golden.

Meanwhile, prepare the blueberry butter: In a bowl, mash the thawed wild blueberries, then mix in the softened vegan butter and confectioners' sugar. Slather it on a freshly baked cornbread muffin!

If you have any leftover butter, you may store it in the fridge for 2 to 3 days.

STREUSEL-TOPPED OATMEAL COFFEE CAKE

YIELD: 12 SLICES
CALORIES: 294 PER SLICE

When I was in my early twenties, I worked in outside sales. I'd work out of various coffee shops, searching for that perfect latte or cappuccino, always pairing it with a delicious item from the café bakery. I was as particular about my coffee cake as I was my coffee. And while my waistline and busy schedule can't really handle nonstop visits to the coffee shop anymore, that doesn't stop me from enjoying a buttery slice of coffee cake with a cup of joe. You will love this healthier vegan twist on a coffee shop classic! The added oats bring fiber and satiety to this fluffy, soft and moist cake. Don't be mistaken; it tastes every bit as indulgent as the café's version, thanks to the sweet cinnamon filling and insanely delicious streusel topping!

Nonstick spray, for pan

1½ cups (360 ml) unsweetened almond milk

1 cup (240 ml) melted vegan butter, divided

¼ cup (50 g) cane sugar

4 tsp (4 g) 100% pure powdered stevia

2 tsp (10 ml) vanilla extract

2 tsp (10 g) baking powder

1 tsp baking soda

2¼ cups (280 g) regular or gluten-free all-purpose flour (I prefer King Arthur Gluten-Free Measure for Measure Flour), divided

1¼ cups (113 g) quick oats, divided

2 tbsp (16 g) ground cinnamon, divided

½ cup (120 g) light brown sugar, divided

Preheat the oven to 350°F (175°C). Spray a 9-inch (23-cm) round baking pan with nonstick spray.

In a large bowl, mix together the almond milk, ¾ cup (180 ml) of the melted vegan butter, cane sugar, stevia, vanilla, baking powder and baking soda. Add 2 cups (248 g) of the flour and 1 cup (90 g) of the quick oats. Mix just until a batter forms; don't overmix, or the cake will become dense.

Pour half of the batter into the prepared pan. Sprinkle the batter with 1 tablespoon (8 g) of the cinnamon and ¼ cup (60 g) of the brown sugar. Pour the remaining batter on top. And, if there's any batter left over in the bowl . . . lick the spoon!

In a small bowl, mix together 4 tablespoons (60 ml) of the melted vegan butter, the remaining tablespoon (8 g) of cinnamon, ¼ cup (60 g) of brown sugar, ¼ cup (31 g) of flour and ¼ cup (23 g) of quick oats. Crumble the mixture over the top of the batter and cover the pan with aluminum foil.

Bake for 30 minutes, then remove the foil and bake for another 30 minutes, or until the streusel is golden and the cake is completely baked through. Insert a toothpick into the middle of the cake. If it comes out clean, it's done.

Serve a slice with your morning cup of joe for an indulgent breakfast!

NUTRITIOUS BLUEBERRY BAKED OATMEAL

YIELD: 8 SERVINGS
CALORIES: 193 PER SERVING

Baked oatmeal is a homey and comforting way to enjoy oats. There's just something about taking traditional oatmeal ingredients, such as almond milk, a little maple syrup and berries, and baking them together that turns oats into an indulgence. Many of my friends and family tell me that they make my "famous" blueberry baked oatmeal every single week. My non-vegan mom and little brother are both blueberry pie lovers and they say it's like eating a healthy blueberry pie! This dish is a great make-ahead meal that you can reheat on busy weekday mornings. It's one of everyone's favorite vegan breakfasts (or desserts) because of how simple, easy and nutritious it is.

---

1 cup (240 ml) unsweetened almond milk

½ cup (120 ml) pure maple syrup

¼ cup (60 ml) melted vegan butter

1 tsp vanilla extract

½ tsp ground cinnamon

1 tsp baking powder

2 cups (180 g) quick oats (see Tip)

2 cups (296 g) frozen wild blueberries

Preheat the oven to 375°F (190°C).

In a large bowl, mix together the almond milk, maple syrup, melted vegan butter, vanilla, cinnamon and baking powder. Then, add the oats and mix until a batter forms. Finally, fold in the blueberries. Pour the batter into a 9 x 11-inch (23 x 28-cm) baking dish and bake for about 45 minutes. The oats will be golden, the blueberries will be bubbly and your kitchen will smell incredible.

Serve immediately or store in an airtight container in the fridge for 3 to 5 days. To reheat and enjoy later, simply portion out a serving into a microwave-safe bowl and microwave for 30 to 45 seconds.

TIP: This recipe is best with quick oats. But if you're in a pinch and don't have quick oats, you can use a food processor to blend regular old-fashioned oats to give them a fluffier texture.

CAJUN-ROASTED HOME FRIES

YIELD: 6 SERVINGS
CALORIES: 106 PER SERVING

While I was growing up, my mom made the most amazing home fries! She knew these boldly flavored pan-fried potatoes were the only way to get me out of bed in the morning. This recipe is a lighter take on my mom's version, but they are every bit as well seasoned, crisp on the outside and soft on the inside. I oven roast the potatoes and caramelized onions to cut out the extra oil and calories. These golden potatoes make the perfect savory side to whatever other breakfast or brunch delight your heart desires.

2 medium-sized russet potatoes, diced

2 medium-sized sweet potatoes, peeled and diced

½ cup (80 g) diced onion

1 tsp chili powder

1 tsp garlic powder

½ tsp salt

¼ tsp freshly ground black pepper

Olive oil spray

Preheat the oven to 425°F (220°C). Line a baking sheet with parchment paper.

In a large bowl, mix together the russet and sweet potatoes and onion. In a smaller bowl, mix together the chili powder, garlic powder, salt and pepper. Add the spice blend to the potato mixture and toss together until the potatoes are evenly seasoned.

Pour the seasoned potatoes onto the prepared baking sheet and spray the top with a little olive oil spray. Bake for 25 minutes. Remove the baking sheet from the oven and use a spatula to flip the potatoes. Bake for another 5 to 10 minutes, or until the potatoes reach your desired crispiness. Serve immediately as a side to any of your favorite breakfast or brunch entrées!

INSANELY SOFT GARLIC ZUCCHINI BRUNCH BREAD

YIELD: 12 SLICES
CALORIES: 125 PER SLICE

Imagine the aroma of freshly baked garlic bread circulating through your kitchen. This tantalizing plant-based loaf is a perfect addition to your breakfast or brunch table. Not only is this savory bread low calorie, it's healthy: The zucchini in the dough makes this loaf super moist while adding some extra nutrients! Between the delicious roasted garlic and herbs and the pillowy soft texture, your taste buds will be in heaven. At only 125 calories a serving, there's no reason why you can't sink your teeth into a slice or two of this delicious garlic bread.

Nonstick spray, for pan

1 tbsp (8 g) flaxseed meal

2 tbsp (30 ml) warm water

1 cup (240 g) grated zucchini

¼ cup (60 g) finely grated carrot

¾ cup (180 ml) unsweetened almond milk

¼ cup (60 ml) olive oil

1 tbsp (14 g) baking powder

1 tsp salt

1 tsp garlic powder

¼ tsp freshly ground black pepper

2 cups (250 g) regular or gluten-free all-purpose flour (I prefer King Arthur Gluten-Free Measure for Measure Flour)

1½ tbsp (13 g) minced garlic

Sea salt

¼ cup (37 g) diced cherry tomatoes

A small handful of fresh basil

Preheat the oven to 350°F (175°C). Spray a 9 x 5-inch (23 x 13-cm) loaf pan with nonstick spray.

Prepare a flax egg: In a small bowl, mix the flaxseed meal with the warm water and set aside to rest for 2 minutes.

In a large bowl, mix together the grated zucchini, carrot, almond milk, olive oil and flax egg. Then, add the baking powder, salt, garlic powder and pepper. Mix well. Finally, mix in the flour until a batter forms.

Pour the batter into the prepared pan and distribute the minced garlic over the top of the loaf as evenly as you can. Sprinkle sea salt to taste over the top. Then, arrange the tomatoes and the basil leaves on top of the dough.

Bake for 50 to 60 minutes, or until golden brown on top. Your kitchen will smell wonderful. Enjoy warm!

HOME-STYLE CHOCOLATE CHIP BANANA MUFFINS

YIELD: 18 MUFFINS
CALORIES: 109 PER MUFFIN

One of my favorite memories as a little girl was baking muffins with my mom on the weekends. These dreamy chocolate chip banana muffins will remind you of all the comforts of home. They're vegan, low calorie and melt-in-your-mouth good. The smell of them alone will have you licking your lips! You will probably have trouble stopping at just one, but luckily, they're just over 100 calories each. Bake these for yourself and the ones you love—no one will suspect they're vegan and everyone will want a bite.

Nonstick spray, for pan

¾ cup (255 g) mashed overripe bananas (about 3 medium bananas)

1 cup (240 ml) unsweetened almond milk

¼ cup (60 ml) melted coconut oil or vegan butter

¼ cup (50 g) cane sugar

4 tsp (4 g) pure powdered stevia (see Tip)

2 tsp (10 g) baking powder

1 tsp baking soda

1 tsp vanilla extract

2 cups (250 g) regular or gluten-free all-purpose flour (I prefer King Arthur Gluten-Free Measure for Measure Flour)

¼ cup (55 g) mini vegan chocolate chips

Preheat the oven to 350°F (175°C). Spray 18 lined muffin molds with nonstick spray to keep them from sticking to the paper.

In a large bowl, mix the mashed bananas, almond milk, melted coconut oil, sugar, stevia, baking powder, baking soda and vanilla. Mix in the flour until a batter forms. Fold in the chocolate chips.

Spoon the batter into the prepared molds and bake for 25 to 30 minutes, or until the muffins have risen and are lightly golden.

Serve immediately or store in an airtight container on the countertop for 2 to 3 days. Reheat in a microwave to enjoy later.

TIP: Not a stevia fan? Swap it out for another ¼ cup (50 g) of sugar (totaling ½ cup [100 g]) to achieve the same sweetness. Don't worry too much; making this swap will add only about 20 calories to each muffin.

GLAZED PUMPKIN BAKED OATMEAL

YIELD: 8 SERVINGS
CALORIES: 180 PER SERVING

You probably know by now that oatmeal is one of my favorite ingredients to include in breakfast recipes. It's an incredible plant-based source of vitamins, minerals and antioxidants. One of the biggest reasons I love oats is that they're a complex carb full of fiber, which will keep you feeling full. There is just something about pumpkin spice flavors that fill your home with warm cinnamon aromas and your heart with cozy autumn feelings. Why wait for fall to enjoy a heavenly pumpkin treat? This is a healthy and delicious "feel-good" food that you can feel great about all year long!

Nonstick spray, for baking dish

1 cup (240 ml) unsweetened almond milk

½ cup (123 g) pure pumpkin puree

¼ cup (60 ml) melted vegan butter

¼ cup (60 ml) pure maple syrup

1 tsp vanilla extract

1½ tsp (7 g) baking powder

1¼ tsp (3 g) ground cinnamon, divided

¼ tsp ground nutmeg

¼ tsp ground cloves

¼ tsp ground ginger

2 cups (180 g) quick oats

¼ cup (30 g) confectioners' sugar

1 tsp softened vegan butter

2 tbsp (30 g) crushed walnuts

Preheat the oven to 375°F (190°C). Spray a 9 x 11-inch (23 x 28-cm) baking dish with nonstick spray.

In a large bowl, mix together the almond milk, pumpkin puree, melted vegan butter, maple syrup, vanilla, baking powder, 1 teaspoon of the cinnamon, nutmeg, cloves and ginger. Then, add the quick oats and mix until a batter forms.

Pour the batter into the prepared baking dish. Bake for about 30 minutes, or until the oatmeal is lightly golden. Your kitchen will smell incredible!

Meanwhile, make the cinnamon glaze: In a small bowl, whisk together the confectioners' sugar, remaining ¼ teaspoon of cinnamon and the softened vegan butter until combined. Add more confectioners' sugar for a thicker icing, but note this will increase the calorie count.

Drizzle the icing over the baked oatmeal after it's cooled for 5 to 10 minutes, then top with crushed walnuts. Enjoy warm!

GRAB & GO OATMEAL RAISIN GRANOLA BARS

YIELD: 10 BARS
CALORIES: 105 PER BAR

Nostalgia strikes again with my craving for oatmeal raisin granola bars. I used to love granola bars as a kid. My mom always bought the prepackaged ones and I never complained. But, as an adult, I try to limit the processed foods in my diet. Processed foods tend to have added sugars, preservatives and other ingredients that our bodies don't need. So, I make my own! These bars are simple, use only eight ingredients and are a wonderfully light and healthy breakfast or snack to power you through the day.

Nonstick spray (optional)
2 tbsp (16 g) flaxseed meal
¼ cup (60 ml) warm water
¼ cup (60 ml) pure maple syrup
2 tbsp (30 ml) melted vegan butter
1 tsp baking powder
½ tsp ground cinnamon
1 tsp vanilla extract
1½ cups (135 g) quick oats
¼ cup (36 g) raisins

Preheat the oven to 400°F (200°C). Line a 9 x 11-inch (23 x 28-cm) baking pan with parchment paper or spray with nonstick spray.

Prepare your flax eggs: In a small bowl, mix the flaxseed meal with the warm water and set aside to rest for 2 minutes.

Next, in a medium-sized bowl, mix together the maple syrup, melted vegan butter, flax eggs, baking powder, cinnamon and vanilla.

Then, add the quick oats and stir. Finally, fold in the raisins.

Pour the granola batter into the prepared pan. Bake the granola for about 15 minutes, or until golden.

Remove the granola from the oven and allow it to cool, then use a knife to divide it into 10 equal-sized bars. Wrap them with waxed paper or plastic wrap to store until you're ready to eat them. They will last for 2 to 3 days on the countertop. To keep them fresher for longer, store them in the fridge for up to a week.

DON'T-SLOW-ME-DOWN LUNCHES

The purpose of lunch is to refuel your energy tank after your busy morning so you can take on the rest of your day. Many people find that when they overindulge or don't eat a balanced midday meal, they end up crashing. Oftentimes, that crash leads to cravings and snacks. My secret weapon to staying satisfied and energized until dinner is keeping lunches light, balanced and tasty! Pulling that off can be a challenge, which is why many of the dishes in this chapter are easy make-ahead meals. I pack in as much flavor as I do veggies and protein—resulting in quick, healthy, plant-based meals that are low on calories and delicious. Whether you're slicing into the Tomato Basil Pesto Pizza (page 61), recharging with the Mediterranean Power Bowl (page 41) or enjoying Crispy Pineapple Fried Rice (page 42), these nourishing meals are going to keep you going until dinnertime!

GREEK-SEASONED LOADED BAKED POTATOES

YIELD: 4 SERVINGS
CALORIES: 345 PER SERVING

Who doesn't love a good baked potato? Not only are they soft on the inside, crispy on the outside and super tasty, but they're also filling and nutritious! When I worked in sales after I graduated from college, I'd run over to the local deli for lunch and grab a baked potato. I loved the process of adding whatever tasty toppings I was in the mood for. Back then, it was often cheese and broccoli. Now that I'm vegan, baked potatoes are still the perfect healthy base for my favorite loaded baked potato toppings. This Greek-inspired baked potato is stuffed with crisp and golden chickpeas, garlicky tomatoes, caramelized onions and a dollop of fresh vegan dill sauce.

---

4 medium-sized russet potatoes

Olive oil spray

2 tbsp (15 g) shredded cucumber

½ cup (120 ml) vegan sour cream

1 tbsp (15 ml) fresh lemon juice

2 tbsp (7 g) chopped fresh dill

1 tbsp (15 ml) olive oil

½ cup (80 g) diced yellow onion

1 tbsp (8 g) minced garlic

1 (15-oz [424-g]) can chickpeas, drained and rinsed

½ cup (75 g) diced cherry tomatoes

1 tbsp (5 g) Greek or Italian seasoning

Preheat the oven to 425°F (220°C). Line a baking sheet with aluminum foil.

Use a fork to poke several holes into each potato. Spray each potato with olive oil spray and place them on the prepared baking sheet. Bake for 35 to 40 minutes, or until the skin is crispy and the flesh is soft. Remove the potatoes from the oven and allow them to cool for 5 minutes before carefully slicing them open.

Meanwhile, prepare the dill sauce: Use a paper towel to blot the excess water from the cucumber shreds. Place them in a small bowl along with the vegan sour cream, lemon juice and dill and stir together. Place the sauce in the refrigerator until ready to serve.

In a large skillet, heat the olive oil over medium heat. Add the onion and garlic and cook for 2 minutes, or until fragrant. Stir in the chickpeas, tomatoes and Greek seasoning. Cook, stirring frequently, for 7 to 10 minutes, or until the chickpeas are golden. Remove from the heat and set aside.

Use a fork to mash the insides of the potatoes, preserving the skin. Add a quarter of the chickpea mixture to each potato. Top each potato with a dollop of dill sauce.

MEDITERRANEAN POWER BOWL

YIELD: 2 SERVINGS
CALORIES: 310 PER SERVING

Lunch is what renews you after your busy morning and trailblazes you through the afternoon. This protein-packed bowl is a nutritious way to give your body the energy it needs without causing a "carb crash" later! It's a plant-based recipe that is simple, easy to prepare and versatile. It gives you the freedom to make it your own by adding your favorite veggies, hummus and spices (calories may vary). In this recipe, I've included my flavorful homemade garlic hummus recipe. Alternatively, you can use store-bought to make this recipe even easier. Serve it fresh or pack it as a meal prep lunch that you can look forward to and feel great about.

For the Power Bowl

Olive oil spray

½ cup (123 g) canned chickpeas, drained, rinsed and patted dry

Italian seasoning

Salt and freshly ground black pepper

½ cup (93 g) cooked quinoa

½ cup (75 g) sliced grape tomatoes

½ cup (75 g) sliced and seeded red bell pepper

½ cup (62 g) sliced cucumber

¼ cup (45 g) pitted black olives

¼ cup (62 g) homemade or store-bought hummus

For the Garlic Hummus

1½ cups (369 g) canned chickpeas, rinsed and drained

2 tbsp (30 ml) olive oil

3 tbsp (45 ml) lemon juice

1 clove garlic

½ tsp cumin

1 to 2 tbsp (15 to 30 ml) water

Preheat the oven to 400°F (200°C).

Line a small baking sheet with parchment paper or aluminum foil and spray it with olive oil spray. Then, add the chickpeas and spray the tops with olive oil spray. Season the chickpeas to taste with Italian seasoning, salt and pepper. Roast in the oven for 20 to 25 minutes, or until they are golden.

If you're using homemade hummus, make it while the chickpeas roast. Add the 1½ cups (369 g) canned chickpeas to a food processor along with the olive oil, lemon juice, garlic and cumin. Process until the mixture is thick and creamy. If the mixture is too thick, add 1 to 2 tablespoons (15 to 30 ml) of water and process it again. You will have leftover hummus, which can be stored in the refrigerator for 2 to 3 days.

When the chickpeas are done roasting, divide them equally among two shallow bowls, along with the cooked quinoa, tomatoes, bell pepper, cucumber and olives. Top the bowls with the hummus and serve.

If you're packing this for lunch, store the chickpeas and quinoa in a separate microwave-safe container, so that you can heat up them up and then top with the fresh veggies and hummus!

CRISPY PINEAPPLE FRIED RICE

YIELD: 2 SERVINGS
CALORIES: 245 PER SERVING

Are you craving something ferociously flavorful for lunch today? Tempted to order Chinese takeout? Give this healthier fried rice a try! The secret to enjoying the savory and enticing Asian flavors of fried rice without breaking your caloric bank account: cauliflower rice! I call this half-and-half rice and you can probably figure out why. It uses half of the white rice that you'd typically use in a serving of fried rice, and pairs it with cauliflower rice. When the two are mixed together, it's hard to tell the difference! This veggie-loaded dish is low calorie, nutritious, satisfying and delicious.

---

1 tbsp (15 ml) olive oil

1 tsp minced garlic

½ cup (83 g) diced pineapple

2 cups (200 g) riced cauliflower

½ cup (55 g) shredded carrot

½ cup (67 g) frozen peas

Salt and freshly ground black pepper

1 cup (170 g) cooked white rice (preferably day-old)

¼ cup (60 ml) coconut aminos or low-sodium soy sauce

In a large skillet, heat the olive oil over medium-high heat. Add the garlic and cook for 1 minute, or until it begins to sizzle.

Add the pineapple and cook for 2 to 3 minutes, stirring frequently. Mix in the cauliflower rice, carrot and peas. Fry for 5 minutes, stirring frequently, and season with salt and pepper.

Finish by stirring in the white rice and coconut aminos. Fry, stirring, for another 5 minutes, or until the rice is golden and crisp (cook longer if a crispier rice is desired).

Serve immediately or store in a microwave-safe container for a healthy meal prep lunch. Great toppings include chives, scallions and sesame seeds.

THREE-BEAN BARBECUE PASTA SALAD

YIELD: 8 SERVINGS
CALORIES: 280 PER SERVING

Have you ever been to a backyard barbecue? Not exactly a vegan's natural habitat, but there are usually some staples that everyone can enjoy. Baked beans and pasta salads always appear at the gatherings I've attended and this recipe combines the best of both worlds. A lot of pasta salads get a bad name because they're soaked in mayo and a bit bland. This flavorful pasta salad is finger-licking good, thanks to the delicious tangy homemade barbecue sauce! The bowtie noodles are tossed in the smoky and sweet sauce and paired with three heaping cups (540 g) of protein-packed legumes, caramelized onions and peppers. Make this pasta salad for lunch or serve it in a big batch for your next get-together. I promise, even the non-vegans will love it!

---

8 oz (226 g) dried regular or gluten-free bowtie pasta

6 oz (170 g) canned tomato paste

¼ cup (60 ml) ketchup

¼ cup (60 ml) water

2 tbsp (30 ml) pure maple syrup

1 tbsp (15 ml) cider vinegar

1 tbsp (15 ml) white vinegar

1 tbsp (15 ml) vegan Worcestershire sauce (gluten free if necessary)

½ tsp garlic powder

½ tsp paprika

½ tsp onion powder

Salt and freshly ground pepper

1 tbsp (15 ml) olive oil

¾ cup (120 g) diced yellow onion

½ cup (75 g) seeded and chopped green bell pepper

1 cup (184 g) canned white navy beans, drained and rinsed

1 cup (184 g) canned pinto beans, drained and rinsed

1 cup (172 g) canned black beans, drained and rinsed

Sliced green onions, for garnish

Cook the bowtie pasta as instructed on the packaging. Drain and set aside in a large pasta bowl.

Meanwhile, prepare the barbecue sauce: In a small bowl, whisk together the tomato paste, ketchup, water, maple syrup, cider vinegar, white vinegar and Worcestershire sauce. Whisk in the garlic powder, paprika, onion powder and salt and pepper to taste. Set aside.

Caramelize the onion: In a medium-sized skillet, heat the olive oil over medium heat. Add the diced onion and cook for 5 to 7 minutes, or until golden and caramelized. Remove from the heat.

Toss the caramelized onion, bell pepper, sauce and beans into the pasta bowl and garnish with the green onions. Serve immediately if you'd like to enjoy this pasta salad warm, or cover and refrigerate for an hour to serve chilled.

TASTY FAJITA VEGGIE WRAP

YIELD: 4 WRAPS
CALORIES: 160 PER WRAP

This veggie fajita wrap is one of my lunchtime go-tos. It's easy to prepare, reheats fabulously and each enormous wrap is only 160 calories, which means you can have two for the price of one! I love filling myself up with veggies at lunchtime. It helps power me through the day and doesn't weigh me down. The golden wraps are filled with seasoned and seared pepper and onion, creamy avocado and spicy salsa.

---

1 tbsp (15 ml) olive oil

2 cups (298 g) sliced and seeded green bell pepper

2 cups (298 g) sliced and seeded red bell pepper

1 cup (160 g) sliced white onion

Salt and freshly ground black pepper

½ cup (120 ml) mashed avocado

1½ tsp (7 ml) fresh lime juice

½ tsp garlic powder

¼ tsp ground cumin

½ tsp chili powder

4 (12-inch [30.5-cm]) store-bought tortillas (see Note)

½ cup (120 ml) store-bought pico de gallo (or any chunky salsa; see Note)

Olive oil spray, to sear wraps

In a medium-sized skillet, heat the olive oil over medium-high heat. Add the green and red bell peppers and onion. Season to taste with salt and pepper. Cook for 10 minutes, or until the onion is browned and the bell peppers are cooked. Remove the pepper mixture from the heat and set them aside.

In a small bowl, mix the mashed avocado with the lime juice, garlic powder, cumin and chili powder. Spread 2 tablespoons (30 ml) of the avocado mixture down the middle of each tortilla. Add one-quarter of the cooked pepper mixture to each tortilla and top with 2 tablespoons (30 ml) of pico de gallo. Wrap the tortillas burrito style.

To sear the filled wraps, spray a large skillet with olive oil spray and heat over medium heat, then fry the filled wraps until golden, about 1 minute on each side. Serve immediately. They taste great paired with salsa!

NOTE: Calories may vary, depending on the brand of tortilla and salsa you select.

TERIYAKI-GLAZED VEGGIE STIR-FRY

YIELD: 2 SERVINGS
CALORIES: 310 PER SERVING

A stir-fry usually appears on my table a few times a week. It's a quick and easy way to cook up a healthy and appetizing meal. The tantalizing smell of this teriyaki-glazed stir-fry will be enough to make your stomach growl! The veggies in this recipe are seared and glazed in tasty teriyaki sauce, and the peanuts bring plant-based fats and protein to this light and lean lunch. The whole recipe will take you less than fifteen minutes and will taste incredible. If you have the calories to spare, this goes great with half-and-half rice!

¼ cup (60 ml) coconut aminos or low-sodium soy sauce

¼ cup (60 ml) pure maple syrup

1 tsp sesame oil

1 tsp cornstarch

1 tsp garlic powder

½ tsp ground ginger

Olive oil spray, for skillet

¼ cup (8 g) chopped scallions

¼ cup (37 g) peanuts

1 cup (110 g) shredded carrot

1 cup (91 g) broccoli florets

1 cup (149 g) sliced and seeded red bell pepper

1 cup (100 g) cauliflower florets

2 tbsp (30 ml) vegetable stock

1 cup (170 g) cooked white rice (optional)

1 cup (100 g) cooked cauliflower rice, prepared as instructed on the packaging (optional)

In a small bowl, make the teriyaki sauce: Mix together the coconut aminos, maple syrup, sesame oil, cornstarch, garlic powder and ginger. Set aside.

Spray a large skillet with olive oil spray and heat over medium heat. Add the scallions and cook until fragrant, no more than about 30 seconds. Add the peanuts and cook, stirring, for 2 to 3 minutes, or until they begin to toast. Then, mix in the vegetables and vegetable stock. Cover and cook for 5 minutes.

Uncover and stir in the teriyaki sauce. Cook, stirring occasionally, until the vegetables are tender, 3 to 5 minutes. Serve immediately.

If desired, serve over half-and-half rice. To prepare the half-and-half rice, simply mix together the cooked white rice and cauliflower rice.

SWEET & SPICY SRIRACHA SHEET-PAN TOFU

YIELD: 4 SERVINGS
CALORIES: 220 PER SERVING

The flavor of this dish is as vivid as the color! Spicy sriracha is mixed with sweet chili sauce to create a perfect combination of sweet heat. This delicious and simple sauce is used as a glaze to marinade the tofu. It's baked on a sheet pan, so you can knock a few things off your checklist while it cooks. Serve this flavorful and lean plant protein over fluffy and filling half-and-half rice and you'll have a boldly tasting, satisfying and low-calorie vegan lunch in minutes!

Olive oil spray

1 (12-oz [340-g]) block extra-firm tofu

4 tbsp (60 ml) sriracha, or to taste

½ cup (120 ml) sweet chili sauce

2 cups (340 g) cooked white rice

2 cups (200 g) cooked cauliflower rice

Preheat the oven to 400°F (200°C). Line a baking sheet with aluminum foil and spray it with olive oil spray.

Press the tofu: Start by draining the water from the tofu packaging, then wrap the tofu in paper towels and use your hands to press until the paper towels soak up the water. Remove the paper towels and repeat the steps until the paper towels can't soak any more water.

In a medium-sized bowl, mix together the sriracha and sweet chili sauce. Cut the tofu into 1-inch (2.5-cm) cubes and toss them in with the sweet and spicy mixture.

Spread the tofu evenly on the prepared baking sheet and bake for 20 minutes. Remove the baking sheet from the oven, use tongs to flip each piece of tofu over and bake for another 15 to 20 minutes, or until your desired crispiness is achieved.

Meanwhile, prepare the half-and-half rice by mixing the cooked white rice and cauliflower rice.

Once the tofu is done baking, serve it over the half-and-half rice immediately.

CREAMY COCONUT CURRY POTATO SALAD

YIELD: 4 SERVINGS
CALORIES: 285 PER SERVING

This is a serious upgrade to the potato salad you're used to. When many people think of potato salad, they envision a tasteless bowl of mush drenched in mayonnaise. This plant-based version is so not that! The sauce alone is enough to wake up your taste buds and will have you wanting to lick your plate clean. This intensely seasoned coconut curry sauce offers the perfect amount of creaminess for the soft yet firm potatoes, and it includes healthful spices: turmeric, cumin and paprika. It's a bright vegan take on a classic dish that you'll want to devour!

---

4 russet potatoes

1 cup (128 g) chopped carrot

1 tbsp (15 ml) olive oil

½ cup (80 g) diced yellow onion

2 tbsp (18 g) minced garlic

1½ cups (360 ml) canned coconut milk

4 tsp (9 g) curry powder

1 tsp ground cumin

½ tsp ground turmeric

¼ tsp paprika

1 tbsp (4 g) chopped fresh parsley

Salt and freshly ground black pepper

Place the potatoes (leave them whole) and carrot in a large pot of water and bring to a boil. Once the water is boiling, cover the pot and lower the heat to a simmer. Cook for about 20 minutes, or until the potatoes are soft but still firm (not mushy). Drain the water from the vegetables and set them aside.

Prepare the curry sauce: In a medium-sized saucepan, heat the olive oil over medium heat. Add the onion and garlic. Cook for about 5 minutes, or until the onion is golden and fragrant. Add the coconut milk, curry powder, cumin, turmeric and paprika. Bring to a boil, then remove from the heat and set aside to cool.

While the sauce is cooling, peel the potatoes and dice them into bite-sized chunks. Transfer the potatoes and carrot to a large bowl and stir in the curry sauce.

Serve warm immediately or store in the fridge for an hour to serve chilled. Sprinkle the parsley on top and season to taste with salt and pepper.

BURRITO BAKED SWEET POTATOES

YIELD: 4 SERVINGS
CALORIES: 315 PER SERVING

Sweet potatoes are one of my favorite foods. Whether they're diced up and roasted, sliced into fries, mashed or stuffed, they're always good and good for you! Sweet potatoes are rich in nutrients and incredibly tasty. When you bake them and load them up with delicious goodies, they make a great base for a balanced lunch. In this book, I've included both a sweet and savory version of loaded baked sweet potatoes. Both are vegan, low calorie, mouthwateringly delicious and wholesome. This savory version is prepared burrito-bowl style. Imagine all of the craveable burrito bowl toppings you love served over smooth and fluffy sweet potatoes. I have a feeling that this is going to be a go-to lunch for you!

4 medium-sized sweet potatoes

1 cup (172 g) canned black beans, drained and rinsed

1 cup (240 ml) store-bought pico de gallo or salsa

1 cup (152 g) diced avocado

2 tbsp (2 g) chopped fresh cilantro

Preheat the oven to 425°F (220°C). Line a baking sheet with aluminum foil. Using a fork, poke holes into the sweet potatoes and place them on the prepared baking sheet. Bake them for 45 to 50 minutes, or until soft. Remove the potatoes from the oven and allow them to cool for 5 minutes, then slice them open.

Top each sweet potato with ¼ cup (43 g) of the black beans, ¼ cup (60 ml) of the pico de gallo and ¼ cup (38 g) of the diced avocado. Sprinkle chopped cilantro over the sweet potatoes and serve immediately.

TIP: If you're bringing these to the office, store the toppings and the potatoes separately when packing. Then, reheat the potato in a microwave and add the toppings once the potato is warmed.

BERRY-LOADED SWEET POTATOES

YIELD: 4 SERVINGS
CALORIES: 315 PER SERVING

In the mood for something "berry" delicious for lunch today? If you've never taken a baked sweet potato, smothered it with almond butter and topped it with berries . . . let me just say, this potato is going to be a game changer for you! This is a well-rounded dish that is sure to satisfy. Sweet potatoes are nutrient-dense superfoods and almond butter is an incredible source of healthy fats and plant protein, while berries are loaded with antioxidants and fiber. Mixing the three together creates a smooth and creamy sweet potato lunch that will make everyone around you "berry" jealous!

---

4 medium-sized sweet potatoes

¼ cup (65 g) almond butter

4 cups (592 g) mixed berries

Ground cinnamon

¼ cup (36 g) crushed nuts, for topping (optional; calories vary)

Preheat the oven to 425°F (220°C).

Line a baking sheet with aluminum foil. Using a fork, poke holes in the potatoes and lay them on the prepared baking sheet. Bake them for 45 to 50 minutes, or until soft and tender. Remove the potatoes from the oven and allow them to cool for 5 minutes, then slice them open.

Serve warm topped with almond butter, berries and a pinch of cinnamon. If you're looking to add a little more protein, serve each potato topped with 1 tablespoon (9 g) of crushed nuts.

TIP: If you're packing these for a meal prep, store the berries, almond butter and potatoes separately. Reheat the potato in a microwave and top with the almond butter and berries once the potato is warmed.

DELICIOUS PEANUT SAUCE & FRESH VEGGIE BOWL

YIELD: 4 SERVINGS
CALORIES: 320 PER SERVING

Peanut sauce is something I slather on just about anything. In fact, I've been known to lick it from the spoon (which is something you should definitely do when you whisk up this yummy sauce). This is a lighter—yet just as tasty—take on traditional peanut sauce because it uses peanut butter powder instead of full-fat peanut butter—less calories but the same amazing flavor! And, it's a great source of plant protein. In this recipe, you will serve this mouthwatering sauce over fresh veggies for a healthy bowl of sweet and spicy goodness. This is a tasty midday meal that will be ready in minutes.

½ cup (24 g) peanut butter powder

¼ cup (60 ml) water

3 tbsp (45 ml) coconut aminos or low-sodium soy sauce

1 tbsp (15 ml) pure maple syrup

1 tsp sweet chili sauce

½ tsp sriracha, or more to taste

1 cup (110 g) shredded carrot

½ cup (35 g) shredded purple cabbage

½ cup (75 g) seeded and diced red bell pepper

½ cup (75 g) seeded and diced green bell pepper

½ cup (62 g) thinly sliced cucumber

¼ cup (12 g) diced scallions

4 cups (680 g) cooked brown rice

Prepare the peanut sauce: In a small bowl, whisk together the peanut butter powder, water, coconut aminos, maple syrup, sweet chili sauce and sriracha. Set aside.

In a medium-sized bowl, toss together the carrot, cabbage, bell peppers, cucumber and scallions. Pour the peanut sauce over the veggies and stir until evenly coated. Enjoy each serving with a cup (170 g) of warm brown rice.

TOMATO BASIL PESTO PIZZA

YIELD: 8 SLICES
CALORIES: 190 PER SLICE

Who says vegans can't have pizza? Who says pizza can't be good for you? Try this recipe and you'll check off your daily greens while enjoying the ultimate indulgent dish. Win-win! It starts with soft-on-the-inside and crisp-on-the-outside homemade pizza crust. Then, spread it with garlicky and fresh homemade basil pesto. Top it with sliced tomatoes and bake to a golden perfection. The best part: You don't need to be vegan to fall in love with a slice of this pizza. In fact, I've had friends and family tell me that this is a step up from a traditional slice!

½ cup (120 ml) unsweetened almond milk

3 tbsp (45 ml) melted vegan butter

1 tsp salt

1 tsp baking powder (only use if baking with gluten-free flour)

2 tsp (8 g) active dry yeast

1 tbsp (15 ml) apple cider vinegar (only use if baking with gluten-free flour)

1½ cups (187 g) regular or gluten-free all-purpose flour (I prefer King Arthur Gluten-Free Measure for Measure Flour), plus more for dusting

2 cups (40 g) fresh basil

½ cup (68 g) pine nuts

2 tsp (10 ml) fresh lemon juice

¼ cup (60 ml) olive oil

2 cloves garlic

1 to 2 tbsp (15 to 30 ml) water (optional)

½ cup (75 g) sliced tomatoes

Prepare the pizza crust: In a microwave-safe bowl, microwave the almond milk for 45 seconds. Transfer it to a large bowl and whisk in the melted vegan butter and salt. If you're baking with gluten-free flour, add the baking powder and mix. Sprinkle the active dry yeast over the top of the mixture and stir just a few times. Let sit for 10 minutes. After 10 minutes, add the apple cider vinegar if you are baking with gluten-free flour. Otherwise, proceed to the next step. Mix in the flour until a thick dough forms, then use your hands to form it into a mound. Be careful not to overwork the dough.

Leaving the dough in the bowl, cover it with a clean towel and allow it to rise for 45 minutes. To make it rise more quickly, you can set it on top of a preheated 350°F (175°C) oven.

While the dough is rising, in a food processor, combine the basil, pine nuts, lemon juice, olive oil and garlic. Pulse on high speed until a creamy pesto forms, adding a tablespoon or 2 (15 to 30 ml) of water if it's too thick. Set aside until you're ready to assemble the pizza.

Once the dough has risen and doubled in size (Note: if using gluten-free all-purpose flour, the dough will rise less, and might be a bit crumblier to roll), preheat the oven to 350°F (175°C) if you haven't already and line a baking sheet with parchment paper.

Roll out the dough on a floured surface into a rectangle about ⅓ inch (8 mm) thick. Transfer it to the prepared baking sheet and bake for 15 to 20 minutes.

When you remove the crust from the oven, increase the oven temperature to 400°F (200°C). Spread the pesto onto the pizza crust and top it with sliced tomatoes. Bake for 5 to 7 minutes, or until the crust is golden. Serve immediately.

NUTRITIOUS & NEVER BORING DINNERS

When choosing to go plant based, many people worry about what they will eat for dinner. Keeping dinner interesting, tasty, nutritious and exciting can be a challenge, no matter what your diet preferences are. This chapter includes an assortment of balanced and delicious dishes that everyone will love. They're all free of animal by-products, simple to prepare and provide a broad range of flavors. The best part is that each serving is under 400 calories.

Whether you have a hankering for Mexican, Chinese, Italian or more, there are plenty of options to please your palate. Some of my favorite recipes from this chapter include the Cheesy Stuffed Bell Peppers (page 71), Rosemary Parmesan Meatballs & Marinara (page 68), Sticky Coconut Fried Rice (page 88) and Sesame Chickpea Lettuce Wraps (page 75). And, don't even get me started on the Mouthwatering Mongolian Lentils & Broccoli (page 64) . . . it's outstanding! Use the vast variety of vegan dinner recipes as a way to ensure that you get to look forward to an appetizing, healthy meal every night.

MOUTHWATERING MONGOLIAN LENTILS & BROCCOLI

YIELD: 4 SERVINGS
CALORIES: 343 PER SERVING

Are you missing the Mongolian beef & broccoli from your favorite Chinese restaurant? Time to get reacquainted with your long-lost lover, because you're going to want to make this recipe over and over. It's half the calories, twice as filling and just as delicious! Instead of beef, I use lentils, which are as flavorful as they are healthy. And, when the broccoli, rice and lentils soak up that sweet and savory Mongolian sauce—you're going to feel like you've entered a vegan paradise!

- ¼ cup (60 ml) low-sodium soy sauce
- 2 tbsp (30 ml) pure maple syrup
- ½ tsp onion powder
- 2 tbsp (30 ml) extra virgin olive oil, divided
- ½ cup (80 g) diced yellow onion
- 1 tbsp (8 g) minced garlic
- 3 cups (273 g) broccoli florets
- 1 tbsp (8 g) cornstarch
- 1 cup (198 g) canned lentils, drained and rinsed
- 4 cups (680 g) cooked jasmine rice
- 2 tbsp (6 g) chopped scallions
- 1 tsp sesame seeds
- Salt and freshly ground black pepper

Prepare the Mongolian sauce: In a small bowl, mix together the soy sauce, maple syrup, onion powder and 1 tablespoon (15 ml) of the olive oil. Set aside.

In a large skillet, heat the remaining tablespoon (15 ml) of olive oil over medium heat. Add the onion and garlic and cook, stirring frequently, for 5 minutes, or until the onion is golden.

Meanwhile, in a medium-sized bowl, toss together the broccoli florets and cornstarch. Once the onion is golden, add the broccoli and cook, stirring frequently, for another 5 minutes.

Add your lentils and Mongolian sauce and stir. Cook, stirring, for 2 to 3 minutes, or until the sauce bubbles and thickens. Remove it from the heat. Serve immediately over a cup (170 g) of rice per serving, topped with scallions and sesame seeds. Season to taste with salt and pepper.

BAKED BLACK BEAN BURGERS WITH AVOCADO SALSA

YIELD: 6 SERVINGS
CALORIES: 160 PER SERVING

In the mood for a juicy burger tonight? My family used to love grilling burgers on the weekends. Now, I skip those meat patties and head for the fiber-filled black bean burgers. They're crisp on the outside, moist on the inside and full of flavor. These southwestern-style black bean burgers are nutritious and the perfect way to crush your burger craving. They can be baked or fried. Take them to the next level with the delicious avocado salsa, and these burgers will make it onto the weekly menu!

---

2 tbsp (16 g) flaxseed meal

¼ cup (60 ml) warm water

1½ cups (258 g) canned black beans, drained and rinsed

1 tbsp (15 ml) olive oil

½ cup (80 g) finely chopped red onion

¼ cup (39 g) corn

¼ cup (31 g) canned green chiles

1 tbsp (8 g) minced garlic

1 tsp chili powder

1 tsp ground cumin

2 tbsp (30 ml) chipotle hot sauce

½ cup (54 g) vegan bread crumbs (gluten free if necessary)

2 tbsp (16 g) regular or gluten-free all-purpose flour (I prefer King Arthur Gluten-Free Measure for Measure Flour)

Nonstick spray (if baking) or olive oil spray (if frying)

1 avocado, pitted, peeled and sliced

¼ cup (37g) quartered cherry tomatoes

1 tbsp (15 ml) fresh lime juice

1 tbsp (1 g) chopped fresh cilantro

½ tsp garlic powder

½ tsp salt

Prepare your flax eggs: In a small bowl, mix the flaxseed meal with the warm water and set aside to rest for 2 minutes.

If you are planning to bake your black bean burgers, preheat the oven to 350°F (175°C) and line a baking sheet with parchment paper.

In a medium-sized bowl, use a fork to roughly mash the black beans. Set aside.

In a large skillet, heat the olive oil over medium-high heat. Add the red onion, corn, green chiles and garlic. Sauté for 5 to 7 minutes, or until the onion is golden. Remove from the heat and set aside.

Mix the sautéed vegetables with the mashed black beans, chili powder, cumin and chipotle hot sauce. Add the flax eggs and stir. Finally, mix in the bread crumbs and flour until well combined.

Divide the mixture into six equal-sized balls and then flatten them into patties about ¾ inch (2 cm) thick.

To bake the burgers, lay them on the prepared baking sheet and spray them with nonstick spray. Bake for about 10 minutes on each side, or until they achieve your desired crispiness.

To panfry the burgers, heat a large skillet over medium heat and spray it with olive oil. Cook the patties for about 5 minutes on each side, or until they achieve your desired crispiness.

While the burgers cook, prepare the avocado salsa: In a small bowl, toss together the avocado, tomatoes, lime juice, cilantro, garlic powder and salt. Serve the burgers topped with equal amounts of the avocado salsa.

ROSEMARY PARMESAN MEATBALLS & MARINARA

YIELD: 6 SERVINGS
CALORIES: 228 PER SERVING

Meatballs and marinara are a timeless and traditional classic that everyone loves. Trust me when I say, you won't miss the beef once you sink your teeth into these juicy and flavorful lentil meatballs. Your family will be amazed at this plant-based and waistline-friendly dish. If you're a spaghetti and meatballs lover, serve these over a bed of cooked spaghetti or spaghetti squash (page 80). Personally, I just love them soaked in homemade marinara sauce. No matter how you serve them, these vegan meatballs are insanely delicious!

---

1 tbsp (15 ml) olive oil

½ cup (80 g) diced onion, divided

1 tbsp (8 g) minced garlic

1 (30-oz [849-g]) can tomato sauce

3 tbsp (45 ml) tomato paste, divided

1 tbsp (3 g) finely chopped fresh basil

1 tsp dried oregano

Salt and freshly ground black pepper

2 tbsp (16 g) flaxseed meal

¼ cup (60 ml) warm water

1 cup (246 g) canned chickpeas, drained and rinsed

1 cup (198 g) canned lentils, drained and rinsed

2 cloves garlic

2 tbsp (7 g) Italian seasoning

¼ cup (25 g) vegan Parmesan cheese

¼ cup (7 g) fresh rosemary

½ cup (54 g) vegan bread crumbs

¼ cup (31 g) regular or gluten-free all-purpose flour (I prefer King Arthur Gluten-Free Measure for Measure Flour)

Olive oil spray, for pan

Prepare the marinara sauce: In a medium-sized saucepan, heat the olive oil over medium heat. Add ¼ cup (40 g) of the onion and the minced garlic. Cook, stirring, for 5 minutes, or until golden. Stir in the tomato sauce, 2 tablespoons (30 ml) of the tomato paste and the basil and oregano. Lower the heat to low and simmer, covered, for 30 minutes. Season to taste with salt and pepper.

Preheat the oven to 400°F (200°C). Line a baking sheet with aluminum foil.

Meanwhile, prepare your flax eggs: In a small bowl, mix the flaxseed meal with the warm water and set aside to rest for 2 minutes.

Prepare the meatballs: In a food processor, combine the chickpeas, lentils, remaining ¼ cup (40 g) of onion, flax eggs, garlic cloves, Italian seasoning and remaining tablespoon (15 ml) of tomato paste and pulse until well mixed. Add the vegan Parmesan, rosemary, bread crumbs and flour. Pulse until combined and use your hands to roll the mixture into about 18 balls, each about 1½ inches (4 cm) in diameter.

Heat a large skillet over medium heat and spray generously with olive oil. Add the meatballs and brown on all sides. Transfer the meatballs to the prepared baking sheet and bake for 12 minutes until they are lightly browned and crisp on the outside.

Serve warm with the marinara sauce.

CHEESY STUFFED BELL PEPPERS

YIELD: 6 STUFFED PEPPERS
CALORIES: 285 PER PEPPER

When I was a kid, the only way my parents could get me to eat vegetables was by smothering them with cheese. Is it just me, or does everything just taste better with cheese? Thankfully, these days, there are tons of delicious vegan cheeses made with healthy plant-based fats, such as cashews. As an adult, I actually crave vegetables (weird, right?), but I still love topping my stuffed peppers with melted vegan Cheddar, and it's the perfect topping for this yummy southwestern dish! Stuffed peppers are as fun to make as they are to eat. The peppers are like a little gift box, and when you slice them open, all the savory goodies spill out. This low-calorie meal is one of my personal favorites and I think you'll fall in love with it, too!

- 4 cups (680 g) cooked brown rice
- 1½ cups (270 g) diced tomatoes
- 1½ cups (258 g) canned black beans, drained and rinsed
- ½ cup (80 g) diced onion
- 2 tbsp (30 ml) chipotle hot sauce, or more to taste
- 1 tsp ground cumin
- 1 tsp chili powder
- 1 tsp garlic powder
- ½ cup (120 ml) vegetable stock
- ¼ cup (60 ml) vegan sour cream
- 6 bell peppers
- ¼ cup (28 g) vegan Cheddar cheese shreds (calories may vary)

Preheat the oven to 350°F (175°C).

Prepare your filling: In a large bowl, mix together the brown rice, diced tomatoes, black beans, onion, hot sauce, cumin, chili powder, garlic powder, vegetable stock and sour cream. Set aside.

Slice the top off each bell pepper and remove the seeds. Place each pepper, open side up, in a baking dish. Use a spoon to scoop the rice mixture into each pepper. Top the peppers with vegan Cheddar cheese shreds and bake for 30 minutes.

Serve immediately.

TIP: Some vegan cheeses melt better than others. I like to spray the top of my vegan cheese with a little nonstick spray and this usually does the trick!

SUN-DRIED TOMATO PESTO & ARUGULA PIZZA

YIELD: 8 SLICES
CALORIES: 145 PER SLICE

While I was growing up, Pizza Night was every Friday in my family! And, just because you're vegan doesn't mean you have to skip it. Instead of basic pizza sauce, I use my famous sun-dried tomato pesto as a seriously flavorful base. You're going to want to slather this stuff on everything! The pesto has a nutty and cheesy flavor due to the nutritional yeast, cashews and pine nuts. These ingredients also provide healthy plant protein and fat, and the peppery arugula is the perfect topping for this appetizing meal.

½ cup (120 ml) unsweetened almond milk

3 tbsp (45 ml) melted vegan butter

1 tsp salt

1 tsp baking powder (only use if baking with gluten-free flour)

2 tsp (8 g) active dry yeast

1 tbsp (15 ml) apple cider vinegar (only use if baking with gluten-free flour)

1½ cups (187 g) regular or gluten-free all-purpose flour (I prefer King Arthur Gluten-Free Measure for Measure Flour), plus more for sprinkling

1 cup (240 ml) water

¼ cup (32 g) raw cashews

4 oz (113 g) jarred sun-dried tomatoes

2 tbsp (16 g) pine nuts

2 tbsp (30 ml) olive oil

1 tbsp (5 g) nutritional yeast

1 clove garlic

½ tsp onion powder

1 cup (20 g) arugula

Prepare the pizza crust: In a large, microwave-safe bowl, microwave the almond milk for about 45 seconds, or until lukewarm, not hot. Whisk in the melted vegan butter and salt. If you're baking with gluten-free flour, add the baking powder and mix. Sprinkle the active dry yeast over the top of the mixture and stir just a few times. Set aside for 10 minutes, then add the apple cider vinegar if you are baking with gluten-free flour. Otherwise, proceed to the next step. Mix in your flour until a thick dough forms. Use your hands to form the dough into a mound. Be careful not to overwork the dough, or it will become tough.

Leave the dough in the bowl and cover it with a clean towel. Allow the dough to rise for about 45 minutes. To help it rise faster, you can set the bowl on top of a preheated 350°F (175°C) oven.

Meanwhile, in a small saucepan, bring the water to a boil over medium heat, then add the cashews. Cover and lower the heat to low. Simmer for 20 minutes.

After 20 minutes, your cashews should be soft and tender. Drain the water from the cashews and pour them into a food processor.

Prepare the pesto: Add the sun-dried tomatoes, pine nuts, olive oil, nutritional yeast, garlic and onion powder to the cashews. Blend on high speed until the cashews, pine nuts and sun-dried tomatoes are broken down and the mixture is blended together. It should take less than a minute. Set the pesto aside.

Once the dough has risen and doubled in size (Note: if using gluten-free all-purpose flour, the dough will rise less, and might be a bit crumblier in texture), preheat the oven to 350°F (175°C), if you haven't already. Then, roll the dough into a circle shape onto a floured surface until it's about ⅓ inch (8 mm) thick. Sprinkle more flour on the dough if it's too sticky to roll. Place the crust on a nonstick metal pizza pan (I like the ones with holes). Bake for 12 minutes, or until golden around the edges.

Remove the crust from the oven and increase the oven temperature to 400°F (200°C). Spread the pesto over the crust. Return the pizza to the oven for another 5 to 7 minutes, or until the pesto turns lightly golden. Remove from the oven and top with fresh arugula. Serve immediately.

SESAME CHICKPEA LETTUCE WRAPS

YIELD: 4 SERVINGS (ABOUT 2 WRAPS EACH)
CALORIES: 282 PER 2 WRAPS

When I was in college and wanted a low-key weekend, I'd order Chinese takeout and watch TV on the couch. Lettuce wraps were a go-to of mine. This recipe is a way healthier (and yummier) option, and the crisp and fresh lettuce is a vessel for crunchy glazed chickpeas and cauliflower. Chickpeas are a nutritious way to pack fiber and protein into your vegan meals, and you know how much I love the nutritious volume food cauliflower! Plus, the sesame sauce alone is something you'll want to lick straight from the bowl. Luckily, this is a simple meal that will taste like takeout, but with a fraction of the calories. So, go ahead, snuggle up and grab your remote.

- ½ cup (120 ml) ketchup
- ¼ cup (60 ml) pure maple syrup
- ¼ cup (60 ml) coconut aminos or low-sodium soy sauce
- ¼ cup (55 g) light brown sugar
- 1 tbsp (15 ml) rice vinegar
- 2 tsp (10 ml) sesame oil
- 1 tsp garlic powder
- 1½ cups (369 g) canned chickpeas, drained and rinsed
- 2 cups (200 g) chopped cauliflower (bite-sized pieces)
- 2 tbsp (16 g) regular or gluten-free all-purpose flour (I prefer King Arthur Gluten-Free Measure for Measure Flour)
- Olive oil spray, for pan
- 1 head romaine or Bibb lettuce
- Sesame seeds, for sprinkling

Preheat the oven to 425°F (220°C). Line a baking sheet with aluminum foil.

In a small bowl, mix together the ketchup, maple syrup, coconut aminos, brown sugar, rice vinegar, sesame oil and garlic powder. Set aside.

In a large bowl, mix together the chickpeas and cauliflower bits. Sprinkle in the flour and toss until everything is evenly coated. Stir in the sesame sauce mixture and pour the chickpea mixture onto a baking sheet lined with foil or parchment paper and sprayed with olive oil spray.

Bake for 20 minutes. Remove the baking sheet and use a spatula to flip the chickpea mixture. Return the baking sheet to the oven and bake for another 10 to 15 minutes, or until the mixture achieves your desired crispness. You will know it's done when it's crispy and golden on all sides.

Serve immediately, using the lettuce leaves as wraps. Try to select the biggest leaves from your head of lettuce to use. Fill each wrap with about ½ cup (82 g) of the chickpea mixture and sprinkle with sesame seeds.

BARBECUE CHICKPEA ZUCCHINI NOODLES

YIELD: 4 SERVINGS
CALORIES: 220 PER SERVING

Here in the South, we love barbecue sauce! Whether it's sweet and tangy or hot and spicy, we tend to slather this stuff on everything. My homemade vegan version of barbecue sauce is easy to whip together and low calorie. The flavors are slightly smoky, mild and sweet, with the perfect amount of zing. And, just because you don't eat meat doesn't mean you can't enjoy this finger-licking-good sauce. Chickpeas are a great plant protein to toss in the sauce. Top a bed of zucchini noodles with it and you've got a low-carb vegan dinner that packs in the taste of the South.

½ cup (120 ml) ketchup
¼ cup (60 ml) pure maple syrup
2 tbsp (30 ml) coconut aminos
1 tbsp (15 ml) chipotle hot sauce, or to taste
1 tsp white vinegar
1 tsp liquid smoke
2 tsp (10 ml) olive oil, divided
¼ cup (40 g) sliced onion
1½ cups (369 g) canned chickpeas, drained and rinsed
4 cups (496 g) zucchini spirals
Salt and pepper, to taste

Prepare the homemade barbecue sauce: In a small bowl, whisk together the ketchup, maple syrup, coconut aminos, chipotle hot sauce, white vinegar and liquid smoke. Set aside.

In a large skillet, heat 1 teaspoon of the olive oil over medium heat. Add the onion and chickpeas and cook for 10 minutes, or until the onion is caramelized and the chickpeas are golden brown.

Meanwhile, in another large skillet, heat the remaining teaspoon of olive oil over medium-high heat. Add the zucchini spirals and cook, stirring frequently, for 2 to 3 minutes. The noodles should be tender but still al dente and not mushy.

Once the chickpea mixture is golden, remove its skillet from the heat and pour the barbecue sauce over the top.

Serve the chickpeas over the cooked zucchini noodles immediately and season with salt and pepper.

LOW-CARB CHEESY CAULIFLOWER CASSEROLE

YIELD: 4 HEAPING SERVINGS
CALORIES: 199 PER SERVING

One evening, I was craving something cozy and comforting for dinner. I thought about the casseroles my mom used to make and how I didn't mind all the hidden veggies in them because they were so deliciously gooey and cheesy. I decided to make a plant based casserole that is just as tasty but without the dairy or meat. And, instead of rice, I opted for cauliflower rice. Give it a try, and thank me later! Seriously . . . you're going to love it (and your waistline will, too!).

- Olive oil spray
- 4 cups (400 g) riced cauliflower
- 1 cup (134 g) frozen peas and carrots
- ¼ cup (58 g) vegan cream cheese
- ¼ cup (60 ml) vegetable stock
- 2 tsp (6 g) garlic powder
- 1 tsp chili powder
- ½ tsp salt
- ¼ tsp freshly ground black pepper
- 1 tsp onion powder
- 1 cup (113 g) vegan Cheddar cheese, divided
- 2 tbsp (6 g) sliced green onions or fresh chives

Preheat the oven to 400°F (200°C). Spray a 9 x 11-inch (23 x 28-cm) casserole dish with olive oil spray.

In a large bowl, mix together the riced cauliflower, frozen peas and carrots, vegan cream cheese, vegetable stock, garlic powder, chili powder, salt, pepper and onion powder. Then, add ½ cup (56 g) of the vegan Cheddar cheese shreds and mix.

Pour the mixture into the prepared casserole dish. Sprinkle the remaining cheese on top of the mixture and lightly spray it with olive oil spray. Bake, uncovered, for 25 minutes. Finish it off by broiling it for 1 to 2 minutes, or until the cheese is bubbly. Top with the green onions and serve immediately.

SLIMMING SPAGHETTI SQUASH PESTO PASTA

YIELD: 4 SERVINGS
CALORIES: 292 PER SERVING

Spaghetti squash is one of the miracles of the food world. It's filling, nutritious and super low calorie. And the fact that this gourd turns into noodles when you bake it in the oven . . . well, that's just the cherry tomato on top! Spaghetti squash is a great way to enjoy "pasta" for a fraction of the calories. In this dish, the silky noodles take on garlicky flavors of vegan basil pesto. PS: Spaghetti squash is also an excellent way to enjoy my homemade Rosemary Parmesan Meatballs & Marinara (page 68).

---

1 spaghetti squash (about 4 lb [1.8 kg])

Olive oil spray

Salt and freshly ground black pepper

2 cups (40 g) fresh basil

½ cup (68 g) pine nuts

2 tsp (10 ml) fresh lemon juice

¼ cup (60 ml) extra virgin olive oil

1 tsp onion powder

2 cloves garlic

1 to 2 tbsp (15 to 30 ml) water (optional)

1 cup (149 g) sliced cherry tomatoes

Preheat the oven to 400°F (200°C). Line a baking sheet with aluminum foil.

Using a large knife, carefully slice the spaghetti squash in half lengthwise, and use a spoon to scoop out the seeds and ribbing. Then, spray the inside with olive oil spray and sprinkle with salt and pepper.

Place the spaghetti squash, cut side down, on the prepared baking sheet. Using a fork, poke three or four holes into the outside of the squash. Bake for 35 to 40 minutes, or until the outside is golden. The time may vary based on the size of the squash. You will know it's done if you can use a fork to gently pull the strands apart. If the strands of the squash don't pull apart easily, bake for another 5 to 10 minutes.

Just before the squash is done baking, prepare the pesto: In a food processor, combine the basil, pine nuts, lemon juice, olive oil, onion powder and garlic. Blend until well combined. Add a tablespoon or two (15 to 30 ml) of water to make the pesto thinner (your preference).

Remove the squash from the oven. Gently pull apart the strands and place them on a serving platter or serve them inside the skin of the squash. Top with the pesto and sliced cherry tomatoes.

GARLIC LOVERS' TOMATO ROTINI

YIELD: 4 SERVINGS
CALORIES: 328 PER SERVING

Are there any garlic and pasta lovers in the building? If so, this is the pasta of your dreams! Tender rotini is tossed in a light and garlicky tomato sauce. This recipe is loaded with healthy vegetables and hearty roasted chickpeas. It's super flavorful, filling and absolutely delicious. And, if you're a leftover lover, you're going to crave this recipe for lunch the next day. In fact, I actually prefer it the next day. Kick your taste buds into high gear and give this easy plant-based dinner a go!

- **8 oz (225 g) dried regular or gluten-free rotini pasta**
- **Olive oil spray, for pan**
- **2 tbsp (20 g) finely chopped onion**
- **1 cup (246 g) canned chickpeas, drained and rinsed**
- **2 cups (60 g) fresh spinach**
- **1½ cups (360 ml) tomato sauce**
- **1 tbsp (15 ml) olive oil**
- **1 tbsp (15 ml) fresh lemon juice**
- **1 cup (20 g) fresh basil**
- **2 tbsp (17 g) finely chopped garlic**

Prepare the rotini as instructed on the packaging.

Meanwhile, place a skillet over medium-high heat and spray with olive oil spray. Add the onion and chickpeas and cook for 5 to 7 minutes, until the chickpeas are golden. Remove from the heat and set aside.

Once the pasta is cooked, drain it and pour it into a large bowl. Add the spinach and stir until it's tender.

Make the sauce: In a food processor, combine the tomato sauce, olive oil, lemon juice, basil and garlic. Pour the sauce into the pasta and add the chickpea mixture. Toss and serve immediately.

CREAMY MUSHROOM RISOTTO

YIELD: 4 SERVINGS
CALORIES: 307 PER SERVING

Risotto is one of those dishes that takes a basic ingredient like rice and makes it taste and feel so special. Traditional risotto is made with white rice, butter, cheese and loads of chicken stock. It also takes a lot of patience. And to be honest, I don't always have that kind of time! But none of this stops me from enjoying one of my favorite Italian dishes. This recipe includes my famous vegan cream of mushroom soup. It's made with vegan butter, flavored with the healthy aromatics garlic and onion and made creamy with a bit of nondairy milk. Instead of white rice, I opt for wild rice, which is a more nutritious option. The duo come together to make a super creamy and indulgent-tasting risotto, in less than 30 minutes.

4 cups (660 g) cooked wild rice
1 tbsp (14 g) vegan butter
¼ cup (40 g) diced onion
2 tsp (7 g) minced garlic
3 cups (210 g) baby bella mushrooms
1 cup (240 ml) unsweetened almond milk (optional)
2 tbsp (30 ml) vegan sour cream
1 tbsp (15 ml) coconut aminos or low-sodium soy sauce
½ tsp salt
¼ tsp freshly ground black pepper
2 tbsp (16 g) regular or gluten-free all-purpose flour (I prefer King Arthur Gluten-Free Measure for Measure Flour)
1 tbsp (6 g) vegan Parmesan cheese

Prepare your wild rice as instructed on the packaging.

In a large pot, melt the vegan butter over medium-high heat. Add the onion and garlic. Cook for 2 to 3 minutes, or until the garlic sizzles and the onion is fragrant. Add the mushrooms and cook for about 5 minutes, or until browned. Stir in the almond milk, if using, sour cream, coconut aminos, salt and pepper. Bring to a boil and then remove from the heat. Sift in the flour, whisking frequently to prevent clumps.

Use a handheld immersion blender to blend the soup until creamy. Immediately pour in the cooked wild rice and serve, topped with the vegan Parmesan cheese.

SHEET-PAN LOW COUNTRY BROIL

YIELD: 4 SERVINGS
CALORIES: 296 PER SERVING

Here in the South, low country boils (and broils) are a way of life. They're easy, filling and finger-licking good. They're perfect for feeding the masses, and there's nothing not to like! This Cajun-seasoned dish includes corn on the cob, golden potatoes, caramelized onions and roasted veggie sausages. Is your mouth watering yet? This is an easy sheet pan supper that will make you feel like you're stepping out of your kitchen and into a southern backyard broil!

---

4 ears of corn, cut across the cob into 1½-inch (3.75-cm)-long pieces

1 lb (454 g) fingerling potatoes, sliced

1½ cups (240 g) chopped onion

12 oz (339 g) sliced vegan sausage

2 tbsp (30 ml) melted vegan butter

1 heaping tbsp (7 g) Old Bay seasoning

Preheat the oven to 450°F (230°C). Line a baking sheet with aluminum foil.

In a large bowl, mix together the quartered cobs, potatoes, onion, sausage and melted vegan butter. Spread the mixture on the prepared baking sheet and season with the Old Bay seasoning. Bake for 20 to 25 minutes, or until the sausage is cooked and the potatoes are golden and browned. Serve immediately.

STICKY COCONUT FRIED RICE

YIELD: 4 SERVINGS
CALORIES: 252 PER SERVING

One of my favorite dishes at Japanese restaurants is sticky rice. It is the mild base for so many enticing flavors. This recipe is one of my favorite ways to enjoy rice. It starts with sautéing your day-old rice and fresh cauliflower florets in vegan butter and coconut milk. It slowly begins to become crispy and golden. Your taste buds will be on overload once you top this sweet and savory fried rice with a heaping serving of fresh scallions.

---

1 tbsp (14 g) vegan butter

4 cups (680 g) cooked jasmine rice (day old is best)

2 cups (200 g) chopped cauliflower

1 cup (240 ml) full-fat coconut milk

¼ cup (12 g) chopped scallions

Salt and freshly ground black pepper

In a large skillet with a lid, melt the vegan butter over medium heat. Add the rice and cauliflower. Cook, uncovered, for about 5 minutes, stirring occasionally, and then pour in the coconut milk. Cover and lower the heat to medium-low. Simmer for about 15 minutes, stirring occasionally.

Remove the lid from the skillet and continue to cook the rice mixture for 20 minutes, stirring every 5 minutes. You'll begin to notice the cauliflower and rice becoming sticky and golden. This is good! For a crispier rice, increase the heat a little. Remove from the heat and top with scallions. Serve immediately. Season to taste with salt and pepper.

FARM-FRESH LEMON SPAGHETTI

YIELD: 4 SERVINGS
CALORIES: 330 PER SERVING

When that basic jar of marinara gets boring, dress your spaghetti noodles with something else instead! One of my favorite ways to spice up spaghetti is with this vibrant and lemony garlic sauce. It's the perfect sauce to tangle up your noodles in. And, there's no need to stop at tomatoes, because the summer veggies in this pasta are a flawless addition to this tasty plant-based dish.

---

8 oz (225 g) regular or gluten-free spaghetti noodles
¼ cup (60 ml) olive oil, divided
2 tbsp (8 g) minced garlic
¼ cup (40 g) sliced onion
2 cups (298 g) diced tomatoes
1 cup (124 g) sliced zucchini
1 cup (124 g) sliced yellow squash
1 cup (70 g) sliced mushrooms
2 tbsp (30 ml) fresh lemon juice
Salt and freshly ground pepper

Prepare your spaghetti noodles as instructed on the packaging. Once cooked, drain and set aside.

Meanwhile, in a large skillet, heat 1 tablespoon (15 ml) of the olive oil over medium heat. Add the garlic and cook for 1 to 2 minutes, or until it sizzles. Stir in the onion, tomatoes, zucchini, squash and mushrooms and cook, stirring occasionally, for 10 minutes, or until the veggies are golden brown. Remove from the heat and mix in the remaining 3 tablespoons (45 ml) of olive oil and the lemon juice, and season to taste with salt and pepper. Stir in the spaghetti noodles and serve immediately.

This recipe reheats well, so feel free to enjoy those leftovers!

FIT & FLAVORFUL TOMATO COCONUT CURRY

YIELD: 4 SERVINGS
CALORIES: 324 PER SERVING

One of my favorite dishes to order when I go to a Thai or Indian restaurant is curry. Nothing kicks your taste buds into high gear like curry sauce that's balanced with the perfect amount of heat and creaminess! Did you know many curry dishes are naturally vegan? This recipe uses coconut milk, which is an excellent source of healthy fat. It's mixed with tomatoes, herbs and spices, and served over a bed of half-and-half rice and broccoli. Half-and-half rice is a combination of white rice and cauliflower rice, and it's a great low-calorie way to enjoy classic white rice with hidden veggies! If you laugh in the face of spicy danger, add more cayenne pepper or some sriracha sauce to your serving.

- 2 cups (340 g) cooked white rice
- 2 cups (200 g) cooked cauliflower rice, prepared as instructed on the packaging
- 2 tbsp (30 ml) extra virgin olive oil, divided
- 1 tbsp (9 g) minced garlic
- ¼ tsp minced fresh ginger
- ¼ cup (40 g) diced white onion
- 2 (15-oz [424-g]) cans tomato sauce
- ¼ tsp ground turmeric
- ½ tsp paprika
- ⅛ tsp cayenne pepper, or to taste
- ½ tsp chili powder
- ½ tsp salt
- ¼ tsp freshly ground black pepper
- 1 cup (246 g) canned chickpeas, drained and rinsed
- 2 cups (180 g) broccoli florets
- ½ cup (120 ml) canned coconut milk

Prepare the half-and-half rice: Mix the cooked white rice and cauliflower rice together and set aside.

Prepare the curry: In a medium-sized saucepan, heat 1 tablespoon (15 ml) of the olive oil over medium heat. Add the garlic, ginger and onion and cook until golden, about 5 minutes. Pour in the tomato sauce and stir. Then, stir in turmeric, paprika, cayenne, chili powder, salt and black pepper. Lower the heat to a low simmer, cover with a tight lid and simmer for 15 minutes.

Meanwhile, heat a medium skillet over medium heat and add the remaining tablespoon (15 ml) of extra virgin olive oil. Once warm, add the chickpeas and broccoli. Cook for 5 to 7 minutes, or until the chickpeas are golden and the broccoli is tender.

Once the curry is done, stir in the coconut milk. You can use a handheld immersion blender to blend the curry together if you'd like, or you can serve it as is. Scoop about a cup (240 ml) of the sauce over the half-and-half rice, chickpeas and broccoli, and serve immediately.

SPAGHETTI SQUASH BURRITO BOWLS

YIELD: 4 SERVINGS
CALORIES: 287 PER SERVING

I love burrito bowls. They are as fun to make as they are to eat. In fact, whenever I'm asked the question "if you could only ever eat one thing for the rest of your life, what would it be?" my answer is always burrito bowls! The reason is that, in one dish, you get plenty of variety and flavor. Follow this recipe and you'll enjoy a big portion of spaghetti squash (one of my favorite nutritious volume foods) topped with delicious black beans, fresh peppers, tomatoes and onion. It's a delectable way to enjoy the flavors of a burrito or burrito bowl without all the calories you get with rice or tortillas.

---

2 spaghetti squash (about 4 lb [1.8 kg])

Olive oil spray, for saucepan

1½ cups (258 g) canned black beans, drained and rinsed

1 tsp ground cumin

1 tsp garlic powder

1 tsp chili powder

1 cup (149 g) sliced sweet pepper or seeded and diced bell pepper

½ cup (80 g) diced red onion

2 tbsp (6 g) sliced scallions

1 avocado, pitted, peeled and sliced

Juice of 1 lime

Salsa, for serving (optional)

Preheat the oven to 400°F (200°C). Line a baking sheet with aluminum foil.

Slice each spaghetti squash in half lengthwise, and use a spoon to scoop out the seeds and ribbing. Spray the cut side of each spaghetti squash with olive oil spray. Place each half, cut side down, on the prepared baking sheet. Bake for about 40 minutes. You will know the squash is done cooking when it's tender and you can easily use a fork to scrape the noodles. If the squash isn't tender and the noodles don't pull apart easily, place the pan back in the oven and continue to bake in 5-minute intervals as needed. Once the squash is done, leave it, cut side down, on the baking sheet until ready to serve.

Meanwhile, heat a small saucepan over medium-low heat and spray it with olive oil spray. Pour the black beans into the saucepan. Season with the cumin, garlic powder and chili powder. Cook for about 5 minutes, or until the beans are warm.

When you're ready to assemble the burrito bowls, use a fork to gently pull apart the noodles, leaving them in the skin of the squash. Top with the seasoned black beans, pepper, onion, scallions and avocado. Drizzle lime juice over the entire bowl. Each squash half is a serving.

If desired, top with salsa.

CRISPY CHICKPEA MEATBALLS & MAPLE BALSAMIC VEGGIES

YIELD: 4 SERVINGS
CALORIES: 262 PER SERVING

Are you craving something golden and fried? Although I usually stay away from fried foods, sometimes the heart just wants what it wants. The key to enjoying fried food is moderation, plus giving it a healthier spin. These falafel-inspired chickpea meatballs are just that! They're crispy on the outside, tender on the inside and super filling. Chickpeas are an excellent source of fiber and vegan protein. These meatballs are versatile and pair well with a variety of sauces, such as marinara, barbecue and my favorite—maple balsamic! Maple balsamic sauce is also a great veggie marinade. In this recipe, I've paired the marinated roasted veggies with the chickpeas for a well-balanced meal!

---

2 tbsp (30 ml) balsamic vinegar
2 tbsp (30 ml) pure maple syrup
2 tbsp (30 ml) olive oil, divided
1 tbsp (8 g) cornstarch
1 tsp garlic powder
2 cups (182 g) chopped broccoli
2 cups (200 g) chopped cauliflower
Salt and freshly ground black pepper
1½ cups (369 g) canned chickpeas, drained and rinsed
¼ cup (40 g) diced onion
¼ cup (27 g) vegan bread crumbs
1 tbsp (8 g) minced garlic
1 tsp ground cumin
1 tsp dried oregano
Olive oil spray, for skillet

Preheat the oven to 400°F (200°C). Line a baking sheet with aluminum foil.

In a large bowl, mix together the balsamic vinegar, maple syrup, 1 tablespoon (15 ml) of olive oil, cornstarch and garlic powder. Use half of the glaze to toss with the broccoli and cauliflower until the veggies are evenly coated. Set aside the remaining glaze for serving. Spread the mixture on the prepared baking sheet. Season with salt and pepper and bake for 20 to 25 minutes, or until the vegetables are cooked and tender.

Make the meatballs: In a food processor, combine the chickpeas, onion, bread crumbs, remaining 1 tablespoon (15 ml) of olive oil, garlic, cumin and oregano. Pulse a few times until the mixture is roughly mixed. Don't overprocess; you want to still see some bits of chickpea in the mixture. Use your hands to pack the mixture to form about twelve 1½-inch (4-cm) meatballs.

Heat a large skillet over medium-low heat, spray it generously with olive oil spray and add the meatballs. Cook until golden on all sides, 3 to 5 minutes per side, and serve with the roasted veggies and remaining maple glaze.

SOUTHWEST TOFU BRINNER SCRAMBLE

YIELD: 4 SERVINGS
CALORIES: 110 PER SERVING

When I was growing up, one of my favorite things to eat was breakfast for dinner. I used to look forward to my mom frying up eggs and home fries in the evening—there was just something about eating breakfast at night that felt like a special treat! This brinner plate swaps eggs for seasoned southwestern tofu scramble for an incredible protein-packed substitute. Instead of deep-frying the potatoes, I bake them, reducing the calories and excess oil. This balanced plate is great on its own and goes well with a side of vegan toast (gluten free if necessary).

---

1 (12-oz [340-g]) block extra-firm tofu

1 tbsp (15 ml) olive oil

1 cup (149 g) seeded and chopped bell pepper

¼ cup (40 g) diced onion

1 tsp garlic powder

1 tsp ground cumin

1 tsp chili powder

¼ tsp ground turmeric

Salt and freshly ground black pepper

Cajun-Roasted Home Fries (page 27), for serving

Prepare the tofu: Drain the water from the packaging. Wrap the tofu in paper towels and use your hands to press until the paper towels soak up the water. Remove the paper towels and repeat the steps until the paper towels can't soak any more water. Set aside.

Heat a medium-sized skillet with the olive oil over medium-high heat and add the bell pepper and onion. Cook, stirring, for 3 to 5 minutes, or until the onion is translucent and the bell pepper begins to brown. Add the entire block of tofu to the pan and use a spatula to crumble it into bite-sized pieces, adding more olive oil as needed. Season the tofu with the garlic powder, cumin, chili powder and turmeric. Cook, stirring frequently, for 10 to 12 minutes more, or until the tofu is crispy and golden. Season to taste with salt and pepper.

Serve with Cajun-Roasted Home Fries.

This tofu reheats well, so feel free to enjoy it for breakfast the next day. You can sear it in a pan again or simply microwave it.

CREAMY LEMON GARLIC PASTA

YIELD: 4 SERVINGS
CALORIES: 343 PER SERVING

I have a confession. When I was a kid, the only way I'd eat pasta was if it was covered in Alfredo sauce. Traditional Alfredo sauce is made with heavy cream, butter and Parmesan cheese. Not exactly vegan or low calorie! I've created a lighter vegan take on this childhood favorite and it is every bit as delicious. Lemon, garlic and a small amount of vegan butter create the perfect smooth and velvety sauce to serve with your pasta. Sneak in the veggies and protein with tender asparagus and golden chickpeas. Feel like a kid again and melt into a bowl of this buttery plant-based pasta!

---

8 oz (225 g) dried regular or gluten-free bowtie pasta

1 tbsp (14 g) vegan butter

2 tbsp (9 g) minced garlic

2 cups (240 g) chopped asparagus

1 cup (246 g) canned chickpeas, drained and rinsed

1 cup (240 ml) unsweetened almond milk

1 tbsp (15 ml) fresh lemon juice

1 tbsp (3 g) cornstarch

Salt and freshly ground black pepper

2 tbsp (13 g) vegan Parmesan cheese

Prepare the bowtie pasta as instructed on the packaging. Reserve about 2 tablespoons (30 ml) of pasta water in the pasta while draining, to keep it moist.

Meanwhile, in a large skillet, melt the vegan butter over medium heat. Add the garlic and cook, stirring, for about 2 minutes, or until it begins to sizzle. Add the asparagus and chickpeas. Cook, stirring frequently, for 5 to 7 minutes, or until the chickpeas are golden and the asparagus is tender.

Add the almond milk, lemon juice and cornstarch to the skillet and stir. The sauce will begin to thicken and bubble. Remove from the heat and season to taste with salt and pepper. Pour the sauce and veggie mixture over the cooked pasta and toss. Season with more salt and pepper.

Top with the vegan Parmesan cheese and serve immediately.

STAUB

SAVORY SOUPS & PLANT-PROTEIN SALADS

Soups and salads are great ways to incorporate veggies into your diet. Lettuce is a volume food, meaning you can eat a lot of it for minimal calories and maximum nutrition, and topping a salad with protein turns it into a satisfying meal. Soups are perfect for enjoying flavorful veggies in a filling and home-style way.

A lot of people think soups and salads are boring, but the recipes in this chapter are anything but! The fresh salads pack tons of punch with bold flavors and plant protein. The savory soups are cozy and filling. So, whether you opt for the Crispy Sesame Miso Tofu Salad (page 107) or dive into the Comforting Veggie Potpie Soup (page 116), your choice will be delicious and nutritious.

SIZZLING TOFU FAJITA SALAD WITH AGAVE LIME VINAIGRETTE

YIELD: 4 SERVINGS
CALORIES: 240 PER SERVING

Whenever I think of fajitas, I think of my little brother burning his hand on the fajita skillet at a Mexican restaurant when we were kids. Speaking of heat—this dish really brings it! It may be light on calories, but it's big on flavor. This bright and vibrant recipe makes a regular appearance on my lunch or dinner table. The fajita peppers are fried with sizzling and seasoned crispy tofu. The pair is served over fresh greens dressed with zesty homemade agave lime vinaigrette. It's a super-tasty and low-carb meal that everyone will love.

1 (12-oz [340-g]) block extra-firm tofu

1 tsp chili powder

½ tsp garlic powder

½ tsp ground cumin

⅛ tsp cayenne pepper

Salt and freshly ground black pepper

¼ cup (60 ml) fresh lime juice

2 tbsp (30 ml) avocado oil

2 tbsp (30 ml) agave nectar

1 tbsp (15 ml) olive oil, divided

2 cups (298 g) sliced and seeded bell pepper

⅓ cup (53 g) sliced onion

4 cups (120 g) chopped romaine lettuce

Prepare the tofu: Drain the water from the tofu packaging. Wrap the tofu in paper towels and use your hands to press until the paper towels soak up the water. Remove the paper towels and repeat until the paper towels can't soak any more water. Then, slice the tofu into 1-inch (2.5-cm) pieces and season with the chili powder, garlic powder, cumin, cayenne, salt and black pepper to taste. Set aside.

Prepare the agave lime vinaigrette: In a small bowl, whisk together the lime juice, avocado oil and agave. Set aside.

In a large skillet, heat ½ teaspoon of the olive oil over medium heat. Add the seasoned tofu and cook for 5 to 7 minutes. Once the tofu is crisp, flip each piece onto the other side and cook, stirring occasionally, for another 5 minutes, or until golden brown on each side.

Remove the tofu from the skillet, then place the skillet back on the heat. Add the remaining 2½ teaspoons (12 ml) of olive oil and then add the bell pepper and onion. Cook for 5 minutes, stirring frequently, until the veggies are lightly charred. Add the cooked tofu back to the skillet and remove the skillet from the heat.

Toss your greens in the vinaigrette and then top with the fajitas and tofu. Serve immediately.

CRISPY SESAME MISO TOFU SALAD

YIELD: 4 SERVINGS
CALORIES: 232 PER SERVING

Bring on the umami! Miso is one of my favorite Japanese flavors. It's also a healthy ingredient to incorporate into dishes because it's rich in vitamins and good for your digestion. Combine it with sesame oil and a little soy sauce, and you've got a dangerously good trio. The sesame miso–seared tofu is crispy and golden. It's topped over a simple salad and dressed with a light homemade sesame vinaigrette. Get ready to put your taste buds in overdrive!

½ cup (120 ml) + 2 tbsp (30 ml) coconut aminos, divided

2 tbsp (30 ml) pure maple syrup

1 tbsp (15 ml) avocado oil

1 tbsp (15 ml) rice vinegar

1 tsp sesame oil

¼ cup (60 g) white miso paste

1 tsp minced garlic

2 tbsp (30 ml) water

1 (12-oz [340-g]) block extra-firm tofu

¼ cup (18 g) baby bella mushrooms

1 tbsp (15 ml) olive oil

4 cups (120 g) chopped romaine lettuce

Prepare the dressing: In a small bowl, whisk together ½ cup (120 ml) of the coconut aminos, maple syrup, avocado oil, rice vinegar and sesame oil. Set aside.

In a medium-sized bowl, prepare the sesame miso sauce for the tofu by whisking the white miso paste, garlic, 2 tablespoons (30 ml) of the coconut aminos and the water.

Prepare the tofu: Drain the water from the tofu packaging. Wrap the tofu in paper towels and use your hands to press until the paper towels soak up the water. Remove the paper towels and repeat the steps until the paper towels can't soak any more water. Slice the tofu into 1-inch (2.5-cm) pieces and combine them with the sesame miso sauce. Add the mushrooms and toss until evenly coated.

In a medium-sized skillet, heat olive oil over medium heat. Add the tofu and mushrooms and cook for 5 to 7 minutes, or until golden brown. Then, flip each piece of tofu onto the other side and cook for 5 more minutes, or until golden on each side. Remove from the heat and set aside.

Pour the dressing over the lettuce and toss. Serve immediately.

CLASSIC & CREAMY CAESAR SALAD

YIELD: 6 SERVINGS
CALORIES: 161 PER SERVING

Everyone loves a Caesar salad. My dad hates vegetables and even he loves this salad! Savory, zesty and super creamy . . . there's nothing not to like. And, since the dressing's base is made with chickpeas instead of egg, it's lower in calories and a great source of protein. Meaning, instead of going "light on the dressing," you can say "more, please!"

---

1 (15-oz [424-g]) can chickpeas, drained and rinsed

2 tbsp (30 ml) water, plus more if needed

1 tbsp (15 ml) olive oil

1 tbsp (15 ml) Dijon mustard

1 tbsp (8 g) capers

3 cloves garlic

1 tsp fresh lemon juice

¼ tsp salt

¼ tsp freshly ground black pepper

6 cups (180 g) chopped romaine lettuce

1 cup (149 g) sliced cherry tomatoes

½ cup (30 g) vegan croutons (gluten free if necessary)

¼ cup (25 g) vegan Parmesan cheese

Prepare the Caesar dressing: In a food processor, combine the chickpeas, water, olive oil, mustard, capers, garlic, lemon juice, salt and pepper and process. Add more water to thin the dressing out to your preference.

Toss the dressing with romaine lettuce, cherry tomatoes, croutons and vegan Parmesan cheese and serve.

GARLICKY BASIL PESTO SALAD

YIELD: 4 SERVINGS
CALORIES: 260 PER SERVING

While I was growing up, basil pesto was something I'd look forward to enjoying whenever I'd visit with my family in Florida. My uncle is Italian and my aunt used to make the most amazing garlic-loaded meals (and still does!). Traditional pesto is made with Parmesan cheese, but thanks to the savory spices and cheesy-tasting nutritional yeast, you won't even be able to tell this is vegan. I made it for my aunt, uncle and cousins last time I was there for a visit and even they approved. That's when I knew how good it was! One of my favorite ways to enjoy it is tossed over a salad, such as this one topped with homemade seasoned croutons. It's a simple, rustic and delicious salad that's a perfect plant-based lunch or a side to any entrée.

---

1 large slice vegan sourdough bread (gluten free if necessary)

Olive oil spray

¼ tsp garlic powder

Salt and freshly ground black pepper

2 cups (40 g) fresh basil

¼ cup (60 ml) olive oil

½ cup (68 g) pine nuts

2 tbsp (10 g) nutritional yeast

2 tsp (10 ml) fresh lemon juice

2 cloves garlic

2 cups (298 g) sliced cherry tomatoes

4 cups (80 g) your choice of chopped greens

Prepare the homemade croutons: Preheat the oven to 450°F (230°C). Slice the sourdough bread into 1-inch (2.5-cm) pieces and lay them on a dry baking sheet. Spray the bread pieces generously with olive oil spray and season with the garlic powder and salt and pepper to taste. Bake for 5 to 7 minutes, or until golden brown. Set aside.

Meanwhile, prepare the pesto: In a food processor, combine the basil, olive oil, pine nuts, nutritional yeast, lemon juice and garlic. Blend until smooth, adding a splash of water if the pesto is too thick (your preference).

Assemble the salad: In a large bowl, combine the cherry tomatoes, pesto and greens. Toss together and top with the croutons. Enjoy immediately.

ZESTY WHITE BEAN CHILI

YIELD: 4 SERVINGS
CALORIES: 220 PER SERVING

Loaded with chiles, healthy legumes and zesty spices—this vegan white bean chili is one of those recipes that everyone will be asking you for. It's super simple and can be made in just one pot. The best part about this dish is that it's protein packed and super filling. Oh . . . and it's beyond delicious! White bean chili is one of those recipes I love diving into during the cold weather months. If you don't mind the extra calories, kick it up a notch by serving it with sliced avocado and/or crushed tortilla chips.

---

1 tbsp (15 ml) olive oil

½ cup (80 g) diced yellow onion

1 tbsp (8 g) minced garlic

2 cups (480 ml) vegetable stock

1 (15-oz [424-g]) can white beans, drained and rinsed

1 (15-oz [424-g]) can pinto beans, drained and rinsed

2 tbsp (30 ml) canned green chiles

1 tbsp (15 ml) fresh lime juice

1 tsp ground cumin

½ tsp chili powder

2 tbsp (2 g) fresh cilantro

In a medium-sized saucepan, heat the olive oil over medium heat. Add the onion and garlic. Cook for about 5 minutes, or until golden but not browned.

Stir in the vegetable stock, beans, green chiles, lime juice, cumin and chili powder. Bring to a boil and then lower the heat to simmer. Cover and simmer for 15 minutes. Remove from the heat and stir in the fresh cilantro.

Serve with your favorite toppings, such as vegan cheese, avocado or crushed tortilla chips.

HEARTY VEGETABLE & BLACK BEAN CHILI

YIELD: 6 SERVINGS
CALORIES: 166 PER SERVING

This is a go-to chili recipe of mine. It's hearty, filling and bursting with flavor. It's made in minutes and I usually have all of the ingredients in my pantry. You probably will, too! The smooth tomato sauce surrounds the seared peppers and onion. The filling black beans provide tons of flavor and protein. It's all cooked together with smoky spices: cumin, chili powder and paprika. The result is a giant cozy pot of chili that will curb everyone's comfort cravings.

---

2 tbsp (30 ml) olive oil

1 cup (160 g) chopped onion

2 tbsp (17 g) minced garlic

1 cup (149 g) sliced cherry tomatoes

4 bell peppers, seeded and chopped

1 (15-oz [424-g]) can tomato sauce

1 (15-oz [424-g]) can diced tomatoes

1½ cups (258 g) canned black beans, drained and rinsed

2 tbsp (14 g) chili powder

1 tbsp (7 g) ground cumin

1 tsp paprika

In a medium-sized pot, heat the oil over medium-high heat. Add the onion and garlic and cook for about 2 minutes. Add the cherry tomatoes and bell peppers and cook, stirring frequently, for 5 to 7 minutes. The peppers will become fragrant. Pour in the tomato sauce, diced tomatoes, black beans, chili powder, cumin and paprika. Stir, then cover the pot. Lower the heat to medium-low and allow the chili to simmer for 30 minutes, stirring occasionally. Remove from the heat and serve.

This chili goes great with crackers, tortilla chips and diced avocado.

COMFORTING VEGGIE POTPIE SOUP

YIELD: 4 SERVINGS
CALORIES: 140 PER SERVING

Nothing says "home, sweet home" like potpie! Y'all know I love a good comfort meal and this soup hits the spot. My bonus mom used to make the most amazing homemade potpie. While it was wonderful, it certainly wasn't low calorie or vegan. If you're a vegan with a craving for a lighter version of potpie, give this recipe a try. It's so delicious, flavorful and filling that you won't even miss the piecrust! This indulgent-tasting soup is secretly nutritious. If you grew up loving homemade potpie, then this soup has your name on it.

---

1 medium-sized russet potato

1 tbsp (14 g) vegan butter

1 tbsp (9 g) minced garlic

½ cup (80 g) diced yellow onion

1 cup (128 g) chopped carrot

1 cup (101 g) chopped celery

3 cups (720 ml) vegetable stock

1 cup (145 g) frozen peas

1 cup (240 ml) unsweetened almond milk

¼ cup (31 g) regular or gluten-free all-purpose flour (I prefer King Arthur Gluten-Free Measure for Measure Flour)

Salt and freshly ground black pepper

Place the potato in a small saucepan and add water until the potato is covered. Bring to a boil and then lower the heat to a simmer. Cover the pot and simmer for 15 to 20 minutes, or until the potato is soft to the touch. Remove from the heat and set aside to cool. Once cooled, gently remove the potato from the pot, remove the skin and use a fork to smash the potato flesh. Don't mash it too well; there should be chunks to give this soup a nice hearty texture.

Next, in a large saucepan, melt the butter over medium heat. Add the garlic and onion and cook for about 5 minutes, or until golden but not browned. Then, add the carrot and celery. Cook for 5 more minutes. Add the vegetable stock, peas and smashed potato. Bring to a boil, cover and lower the heat to low. Cook for 5 minutes.

Remove the pot from the heat and add the almond milk. Stir, then sift in the flour while whisking the soup to prevent clumps.

Allow the soup to cool and thicken for 5 to 10 minutes, then serve warm. Season to taste with salt and pepper.

THERE'S ALWAYS ROOM FOR DESSERT

My name is Jill and I have a sweet tooth! A ravenous and killer sweet tooth. I've talked to you guys about my diet before, and there's a reason that I'm so motivated every day to eat healthy and fill up on clean and whole foods. It's because I'm saving room for dessert! I eat dessert daily and you can, too. And, just because you're vegan (or gluten free), doesn't mean you can't enjoy sweets like my Super-Moist Lemon Loaf (page 135) or Mama's Maple Butter Crescent Rolls (page 123).

Manage your calories and portions, make great choices during your day and choose one of these delightful and healthy(ish) treats to sink your teeth into. I try to incorporate some nutritious elements into this crave-worthy final course. Whether you are cozying up with Chocolate Chip Banana Cookies (page 131), enjoying an Autumn Apple Cider Donut (page 136) or a slice of Healthy Oatmeal Carrot Cake (page 139), these desserts are always delicious, plant based, can be made gluten free and are lighter takes on their traditional counterparts. So go ahead . . . have your dessert and eat it, too.

SNICKERDOODLE COOKIES

YIELD: 18 COOKIES
CALORIES: 116 PER COOKIE

Whenever I bake these cinnamon-sugared cookies for friends and family, they disappear faster than I can say the word snickerdoodle! I make these chewy and soft cookies every year at Christmas. They're sugary, buttery and oh so moist. Have you ever met anyone who doesn't like a snickerdoodle cookie? Neither have I! Serve a batch of these to your friends and family or bake them and keep them to yourself. They taste amazing served with a nice cold glass of oat or almond milk and a good TV show.

---

2 tbsp (16 g) flaxseed meal

¼ cup (60 ml) warm water

1½ tsp (4 g) ground cinnamon, divided

¾ cup (150 g) + 3 tbsp (38 g) cane sugar, divided

½ cup (120 ml) melted vegan butter

1 tsp vanilla extract

1 tsp baking powder

½ tsp cream of tartar

1¼ cups (156 g) regular or gluten-free all-purpose flour (I prefer King Arthur Gluten-Free Measure for Measure Flour)

Preheat the oven to 375°F (190°C). Line a cookie sheet with parchment paper.

Prepare your flax eggs: In a small bowl, mix the flaxseed meal with the warm water and set aside to rest for 2 minutes.

Prepare the topping: In a small bowl, whisk together ½ teaspoon of the cinnamon and 3 tablespoons (38 g) of the cane sugar. Set aside.

In a large bowl, mix together the melted vegan butter, remaining ¾ cup (150 g) of cane sugar, vanilla, baking powder, remaining teaspoon of cinnamon and the cream of tartar. Add the flax eggs and mix. Then mix in the flour just until combined.

Use a tablespoon (15-ml)-sized measure to scoop out the dough, form each scoop into a ball using your hands and then toss it into the cinnamon-sugar topping. Place the balls about 1 inch (2.5 cm) apart on the prepared cookie sheet and bake for about 12 minutes. You will know they are done when they are slightly golden on the bottom.

Remove from the oven and allow the cookies to cool for 5 minutes before serving.

MAMA'S MAPLE BUTTER CRESCENT ROLLS

YIELD: 24 ROLLS
CALORIES: 91 PER ROLL

My mom was a single mom and taught me to be independent, strong and fearless. I never went without and she always had dinner (and dessert) on the table. One of her gourmet staples was canned crescent rolls, drizzled with honey butter. Butter and honey aren't vegan, and canned dough is highly processed. But that doesn't stop me from making a homemade batch of vegan crescent rolls and drizzling them with vegan maple butter. These crescents are baked to golden and soft perfection, and you won't even miss that adorable dough guy in the chef's hat my mom loved so much. When you soak them in the melty maple butter . . . well, let's just say, you'll have trouble stopping at one.

---

1 cup (240 ml) unsweetened almond milk

7 tbsp (100 ml) melted vegan butter, divided

5 tbsp (75 ml) pure maple syrup, divided

½ tsp salt

1 tbsp (9 g) active dry yeast

2½ cups (313 g) regular all-purpose flour

In a large, microwave-safe bowl, microwave the almond milk for about 30 seconds, or until warm but not hot.

Mix in 4 tablespoons (60 ml) of the melted vegan butter, 2 tablespoons (30 ml) of the maple syrup and the salt. Sprinkle the active dry yeast evenly over the top of the mixture, stir once or twice and let it sit for 10 minutes. Mix in the flour until the dough is too thick to mix, then use your hands to form the dough into a round mound. Cover the bowl with a clean towel and let the dough rise for 1 hour. Optionally, set the bowl of dough on top of a preheated 350°F (175°C) oven to make it rise faster.

Once the dough has risen, if you haven't already, preheat the oven to 350°F (175°C). Line a baking sheet with parchment paper.

On a floured surface, roll out the dough into a rectangle about ⅓ inch (8 mm) thick. Slice the dough into two dozen 4- to 5-inch (10- to 12.5-cm)-long triangles and use your fingers to stretch 2 corners of each triangle. Loosely roll the triangles to create a "crescent" shape. Bake for about 15 minutes, or until the crescents have risen and are lightly golden.

Meanwhile, in a small bowl, whisk together the remaining 3 tablespoons (45 ml) of maple syrup and 3 tablespoons (45 ml) of melted vegan butter to make the maple butter. Serve the crescents on a large serving platter and either drizzle the maple butter over the top of them, brush each roll individually or serve the maple butter on the side for dipping.

HEAVENLY LIGHT BLACKBERRY CAKE

YIELD: 12 SERVINGS
CALORIES: 204 PER SERVING

Life's too short to not eat cake! And this cake is one you won't want to miss. A perfect cake is moist, delicate, soft and fluffy. It's sweet, but not too sweet. It's iced, but not so much that it overwhelms the cake. This cake is everything I just mentioned and more. Typical cakes are loaded with tons of butter, sugar and cow's milk. This lighter version is melt-in-your-mouth good, and each slice is just over 200 calories. So, go ahead . . . indulge away!

Nonstick spray, for pan

1 cup (240 ml) unsweetened almond milk

½ cup (100 g) cane sugar

¼ cup (60 ml) melted vegan butter

2 tsp (10 ml) vanilla extract, divided

1 tsp baking powder

1 tsp baking soda

½ tsp ground cinnamon

2¼ cups (281 g) regular or gluten-free all-purpose flour (I prefer King Arthur Gluten-Free Measure for Measure Flour)

1 cup (130 g) frozen or fresh blackberries

1 cup (120 g) confectioners' sugar

1 tbsp (15 ml) melted coconut oil

Preheat the oven to 375°F (190°C). Spray a 9 x 5-inch (23 x 13-cm) loaf pan with nonstick spray.

In a large bowl, whisk together the almond milk, cane sugar, melted vegan butter, 1 teaspoon of the vanilla, the baking powder, baking soda and cinnamon. Then, whisk in the flour just until a batter forms. Be careful not to overmix, or the cake will be tough. Fold in the blackberries. Pour the batter into the prepared pan. Bake for 40 to 50 minutes, or until the cake is lightly golden on top. Remove it from the oven and insert a toothpick into the middle of the loaf. If it comes out clean, it's done. If not, continue to bake for 3- to 5-minute intervals until done.

Meanwhile, make the glaze: In a medium-sized bowl, using an electric hand mixer, mix together the confectioners' sugar, coconut oil and the remaining teaspoon of vanilla.

When the cake is done, remove it from the oven, remove it from the loaf pan and allow it to cool on a wire rack for 5 to 10 minutes. Then, pour the glaze over the top of the loaf and serve warm.

QUICK & EASY OPEN-FACED APPLE PIE

YIELD: 8 SLICES
CALORIES: 256 PER SLICE

Baked apple pie is great for any occasion. Whether it's the Fourth of July or Christmas morning, there's always a place for apple pie on the table. One of my brothers is an apple pie fiend and I like to bake him a fresh one for special occasions, or just because. To keep it light, I've taken my classic recipe and made it "open-faced," and the results look, smell and taste amazing. The tender and golden piecrust and the cinnamon apples are irresistible! If you're someone who likes an apple pie with a bite, choose Granny Smith apples for this recipe. And, if you're like me and love a sweeter take, grab some Honeycrisps!

---

4 medium-sized apples

1⅔ cups (203 g) + 2 tbsp (16 g) regular or gluten-free all-purpose flour (I prefer King Arthur Gluten-Free Measure for Measure Flour), divided, plus more if needed

½ cup (100 g) cane sugar

2 tbsp (30 g) vegan butter

1 tbsp (15 ml) fresh lemon juice

1 tsp ground cinnamon

¼ tsp ground nutmeg

½ cup (120 ml) unsweetened almond milk

3 tbsp (45 ml) melted coconut oil

1½ tsp (7 g) baking powder

½ tsp salt

Peel, core and slice the apples about ⅛ inch (3 mm) thick. Place them in a large bowl and toss in 2 tablespoons (16 g) of the flour. Stir in the sugar, vegan butter, lemon juice, cinnamon and nutmeg. Set the apples in the fridge.

Prepare your dough: In a large bowl, mix together the almond milk, coconut oil, baking powder and salt. Then, add the remaining 1⅔ cups (203 g) of flour and mix until a thick dough forms. When you can't stir the dough anymore, use your fingers to gently work the dough until all the flour is integrated. Be careful not to overwork your dough. Form the dough into a mound. Use a clean towel to cover the dough in the bowl and set it aside for about 10 minutes.

Preheat the oven to 350°F (175°C).

Roll the dough into a 12- to 14-inch (30.5- to 35.5-cm) circle, adding more flour if the dough is sticky. Lay the dough over a 9- or 10-inch (23- or 25.5-cm) pie dish and use your fingers to press it into the dish. There should be enough dough that it hangs over the edges of the dish. Add the apple slices. I stacked my apple slices neatly, but if you don't have the time or patience for that, feel free to just toss them in! Fold the edges of the dough over the apples to create a border. Bake for about 40 minutes, or until the piecrust is lightly golden. Remove the pie from the oven, allow it to cool for 5 minutes and enjoy warm by itself or with your favorite nondairy ice cream.

FLUFFY COCONUT CAKE

YIELD: 12 SLICES
CALORIES: 287 PER SLICE

There are few things in life as luxurious and special as a slice of cake. Coconut cake is a staple here in the South. It's dense, moist, tender and delicious. The non-vegan version uses dairy, eggs and a little too much sugar! This lighter vegan version is just as decadent, delicious, pillowy soft and perfectly sweet. One of the healthiest ingredients in this cake is the coconut milk. It's also what makes this cake so moist and sweet without having to overdo it on the butter or sugar. My famous homemade vegan cream cheese icing is the perfect topping for this dessert.

Nonstick cooking spray, for pan

2 tbsp (16 g) flaxseed meal

¼ cup (60 ml) warm water

1½ cups (360 ml) canned full-fat coconut milk

¾ cup (150 g) cane sugar

1 tbsp (15 ml) fresh lemon juice

2 tsp (9 g) baking powder

1 tsp baking soda

2 tsp (10 ml) vanilla extract

1½ cups (187 g) regular or gluten-free all-purpose flour (I prefer King Arthur Gluten-Free Measure for Measure Flour)

½ cup (60 g) coconut flour

2 oz (57 g) vegan cream cheese

¾ cup (90 g) confectioners' sugar

2 tbsp (28 g) softened vegan butter

¼ cup (23 g) unsweetened shredded coconut

Preheat the oven to 350°F (175°C). Spray a 9-inch (23-cm) round springform cake pan with nonstick cooking spray.

Prepare your flax eggs: In a small bowl, mix the flaxseed meal with the warm water and set aside to rest for 2 minutes.

In a large mixing bowl, mix together the coconut milk, cane sugar, flax eggs, lemon juice, baking powder, baking soda and vanilla. Whisk in the all-purpose and coconut flours until a smooth batter forms.

Pour the batter into the prepared baking pan and bake for 35 to 40 minutes, or until completely cooked through the middle (test the center with a toothpick) and the top is golden brown.

Meanwhile, make the icing: In a medium-sized bowl, use an electric hand mixer to mix together the vegan cream cheese, confectioners' sugar and vegan butter. Set aside.

Once the cake is done, remove it from the oven and allow it to cool in the pan. Once cooled, remove the cake from the pan and then spread the cream cheese icing over it. Sprinkle with shredded coconut and serve.

CHOCOLATE CHIP BANANA COOKIES

YIELD: 24 COOKIES
CALORIES: 87 PER COOKIE

One of my little brothers is a chocolate chip cookie connoisseur, and this recipe is inspired by him! Homemade cookies can be time-consuming to prepare—and loaded with butter and sugar. Luckily, I'm pretty good at shortcuts and making lighter versions of classic favorites. Here, the yummy flavor of banana bread and chocolate combine in a remarkably soft and moist cookie. The key to making them perfectly sweet is to use really ripe bananas (as if making a banana bread). The result is a chocolate chip banana cookie that's a bit healthier than its non-vegan alternative, but every bit as scrumptious!

---

1 cup (340 g) mashed overripe bananas

⅔ cup (132 g) cane sugar

3 tbsp (45 ml) melted vegan butter

¼ cup (60 ml) unsweetened almond milk

1 tsp vanilla extract

1 tsp baking powder

½ tsp salt

1¼ cups (156 g) regular or gluten-free all-purpose flour (I prefer King Arthur Gluten-Free Measure for Measure Flour)

½ cup (60 g) coconut flour

¼ cup (42 g) mini vegan chocolate chips

Preheat the oven to 400°F (200°C). Line a baking sheet with parchment paper.

In a large bowl, mix together the mashed bananas, sugar, melted vegan butter, almond milk, vanilla, baking powder and salt. Once combined, whisk in the all-purpose and coconut flours. A thick dough should form. Fold in the chocolate chips and use a tablespoon (15-ml)-sized measure to drop the batter about 1 inch (2.5 cm) apart onto the prepared baking sheet. There should be 24 cookies.

Bake for 12 to 15 minutes, or until the cookies are lightly golden on top and slide easily off the paper. Serve immediately with a cold glass of almond milk or store in an airtight container on the counter for 2 to 3 days.

6-INGREDIENT BLACKBERRY CRUMBLE

YIELD: 8 SERVINGS
CALORIES: 180 PER SERVING

Baking berries (and other fruit) is a great way to enhance their natural sweetness without needing to add sugar. This recipe tops juicy and bubbling blackberries with lightly sweet and buttery oatmeal crumble. Oatmeal is a great ingredient to use in light and low-calorie baking! If you're craving something delicious to tuck into tonight, give this easy and nutritious vegan dessert a try. Oh, and be ready for your senses to be on overload as the heavenly aroma of baking berries and oats circulates through your home.

Nonstick spray, for dish

5 cups (650 g) fresh or frozen blackberries

2 tbsp (15 g) regular or gluten-free all-purpose flour (I prefer King Arthur Gluten-Free Measure for Measure Flour)

1 cup (90 g) quick oats

¼ cup (50 g) cane sugar

¼ cup (60 ml) melted coconut oil

1 tsp ground cinnamon

Preheat the oven to 375°F (190°C). Spray a casserole or pie dish with nonstick spray.

In a large bowl, mix the blackberries with the flour. Pour the flour-coated blackberries into the prepared dish.

In a smaller bowl, mix together the oats, sugar, coconut oil and cinnamon until a crumble forms.

Sprinkle the crumble evenly over the top of the blackberries. Bake for 35 to 40 minutes, or until the crumble is golden and the blackberries are bubbling.

Serve warm.

SUPER-MOIST LEMON LOAF

YIELD: 10 SERVINGS
CALORIES: 215 PER SERVING

This mouthwatering vegan lemon loaf is my most popular recipe! I make it for special occasions, and when I serve it to non-vegans, they end up begging for the recipe and licking their plate clean. This is one of those cakes people rave about because it literally melts in your mouth. The tender and sensationally soft cake is topped with vegan cream cheese icing. This recipe is simple, delicious and low calorie. Next time you have an occasion to bake for (or next time you want to bake something, period), give this a try! I can guarantee that this will be your new go-to vegan cake.

Nonstick baking spray, for pan

1 cup (240 ml) unsweetened almond milk

½ cup (120 ml) fresh lemon juice

¼ cup (60 ml) melted vegan butter

1 cup (200 g) cane sugar (see Tip)

1 tsp vanilla extract

1 tsp baking soda

1½ tsp (7 g) baking powder

2¼ cups (281 g) regular or gluten-free all-purpose flour (I prefer King Arthur Gluten-Free Measure for Measure Flour)

¾ cup (90 g) confectioners' sugar

2 tbsp (28 g) softened vegan butter

2 oz (57 g) vegan cream cheese

Preheat the oven to 375°F (190°C). Spray a 9 x 5-inch (23 x 13-cm) loaf pan with nonstick baking spray.

In a large bowl, mix together the almond milk, lemon juice, melted vegan butter, cane sugar and vanilla. Then, quickly mix in the baking soda and baking powder. Add the flour immediately and stir just until a batter forms. Be careful not to overmix. It might look a little lumpy, but this is okay!

Pour the batter into the prepared pan and bake for 40 to 45 minutes, or until lightly golden on top. Remove the loaf from the oven and allow it to cool in the pan for 5 to 10 minutes.

Meanwhile, make the vegan cream cheese icing: In a medium-sized bowl, using an electric hand mixer, mix together the confectioners' sugar, softened vegan butter and cream cheese. Store it in the fridge until the loaf is done baking.

When the loaf has cooled, remove it from the pan, then spread the vegan cream cheese icing over the loaf while it's still slightly warm. Serve immediately.

TIP: For an even lower-calorie loaf, replace the cup (200 g) of cane sugar with ¼ cup (50 g) of cane sugar plus 4 teaspoons (15 g) of powdered stevia.

AUTUMN APPLE CIDER DONUTS

YIELD: 18 DONUTS
CALORIES: 130 PER DONUT

I love fall. I love when the leaves begin to change and the temperature starts to drop. While growing up, one of my favorite things to do in autumn was to take my brother to the local pumpkin patch. Sure, the pumpkins were great, but the most enticing part of that trip was the fresh and warm apple cider donuts that were sold there. If you've never had an apple cider donut, you're missing out. But now, you don't have to! And, whereas the ones at the farm were usually greasy and fried (and delicious), these are vegan donuts you can feel great about. These cinnamon-sugared treats are only 130 calories apiece, which makes them much lighter than the traditional version, but every bit as tasty!

---

2 tbsp (16 g) flaxseed meal

¼ cup (60 ml) warm water

Nonstick baking spray, for pan

1 cup (240 ml) unsweetened almond milk

½ cup (62 g) coconut sugar

½ cup (100 g) cane sugar, divided

½ cup (120 ml) unsweetened applesauce

¼ cup (60 ml) melted vegan butter

2 tbsp (30 ml) cider vinegar

1½ tsp (7 g) baking powder

1 tsp baking soda

2 tsp (10 g) ground cinnamon, divided

½ tsp salt

2 cups (180 g) oat flour

Prepare your flax eggs: In a small bowl, mix the flaxseed meal with the warm water and set aside to rest for 2 minutes.

Preheat the oven to 375°F (190°C). Spray 18 donut molds with nonstick baking spray

In a large bowl, mix together the almond milk, coconut sugar, ¼ cup (50 g) of the cane sugar, the applesauce, melted vegan butter, cider vinegar, baking powder, baking soda, 1 teaspoon of the cinnamon and the salt. Once combined, mix in the flax eggs. Then, mix in the oat flour until the batter is silky and smooth. Pour the batter into the prepared donut molds and bake for 25 to 30 minutes, or until golden.

Meanwhile, in a small bowl, mix together the remaining teaspoon of cinnamon and ¼ cup (50 g) of cane sugar. Remove the donuts from the oven and immediately toss in the cinnamon-sugar mixture. Serve warm.

HEALTHY OATMEAL CARROT CAKE

YIELD: 12 SERVINGS
CALORIES: 241 PER SERVING

Carrot cake is the ultimate indulgence. The perfect carrot cake should be super moist, dense and over-the-top delicious. This recipe delivers all that, while incorporating a few healthier swaps. The carrots add moisture, density and weight to this rich cake. The oats and flaxseeds add fiber and fluffiness. When you spread the cake with vegan cream cheese icing, it's a plant based dessert you won't be able to resist. This is a healthier version of a classic, made without dairy, eggs or refined flour. And, let me tell you, it'll knock your socks off!

---

2 tbsp (16 g) flaxseed meal

¼ cup (60 ml) warm water

Nonstick baking spray, for pan

1 cup (240 ml) unsweetened almond milk

¾ cup (180 ml) pure maple syrup

1 cup (110 g) finely grated carrot

¼ cup (60 ml) melted vegan butter

1½ tsp (7 g) baking powder

1 tsp baking soda

1 tsp vanilla extract

1 tsp ground cinnamon

1 cup (90 g) quick oats

2 cups (180 g) oat flour

2 tbsp (28 g) softened vegan butter

2 oz (57 g) vegan cream cheese

¾ cup (90 g) confectioners' sugar

Prepare your flax eggs: In a small bowl, mix the flaxseed meal with the warm water and set aside to rest for 2 minutes.

Preheat the oven to 375°F (190°C). Spray an 8- or 9-inch (20- or 23-cm) round cake pan with nonstick baking spray.

In a large bowl, whisk together the almond milk, maple syrup, grated carrot, melted vegan butter, flax eggs, baking powder, baking soda, vanilla and cinnamon. Then, add the quick oats and oat flour. Whisk until well combined and then pour the batter into the prepared pan. Bake for about 40 minutes, or until you can stick a toothpick into the center of the cake and it comes out clean.

Meanwhile, prepare the cream cheese icing: In a medium-sized bowl, using an electric hand mixer, mix together the softened vegan butter, cream cheese and confectioners' sugar. Set aside until you're ready to serve the cake.

Once the cake is done, remove it from the oven, allow it to cool for 5 to 10 minutes and spread the cream cheese icing over the top.

ACKNOWLEDGMENTS

I'D LIKE TO THANK GOD, FOR WITHOUT HIM, NONE OF THIS WOULD BE POSSIBLE.

TO MY FRIENDS & FAMILY

It's pretty safe to say that 2020 was a challenging year for the entire world. And as I celebrated one of my greatest accomplishments—this book—I also faced one of my greatest personal losses. To my sweet and wonderful family and friends, you guys were my recipe testers, cheerleaders, errand runners, brainstorming partners, shoulders to cry on and prayer warriors. Thank you for being there. Your virtual and physical presence carried my heart. You lifted my spirits . . . and some of you even lifted my moving boxes. You helped me pick up the pieces and made me whole again.

I don't know how I got so lucky to have you all. And I am beyond excited to share the joy of publishing my first book with you.

TO MY READERS

You guys are my inspiration and my motivation. The fact that you take time out of your day to visit my blog, to try my recipes and share them with your families is a true honor. It is my greatest pleasure and joy in what I do. Nothing makes my day like receiving a photo of you guys enjoying one of my recipes. I started sharing my recipes to help others and make them smile, and it turns out, you guys have helped me and made me smile. Thank you for following along on this journey with me and for letting me be a little part of your lives.

TO THE TEAM AT REVOLUTION STUDIOS

Your dedication to this project went above and beyond what's typical. Your photos captured the heart and soul of my recipes and your friendship touched my heart. I couldn't have done it without you!

TO THE TEAM AT EUFLORIA (FORMERLY WILDFLOWER DESIGN WORKS)

Eufloria, your props and staging helped spotlight my recipes in a beautiful way. Beyond that, your assistance (taste testing, running out for ingredients and just being there) and love was more appreciated than words will ever describe. I feel beyond blessed to have such an incredible family and "cookbook team" supporting me.

TO THE GALS AT 90 DEGREE DESIGN

Your web design, logo design and branding brought my little recipe blog to life. And more importantly, you are three great friends.

TO PAGE STREET PUBLISHING

Caitlin, when I first received your email, I couldn't stop pinching myself. It is a lifelong dream of mine to be an author. I will never forget the first time we spoke on the phone, the day when I realized that my recipes could one day be published. To you and the entire team at Page Street Publishing, thank you for taking a shot on me. Thank you for being so wonderful to work with throughout this process. For believing in me and for making my dreams come true.

ABOUT THE AUTHOR

JILLIAN (JILL) GLENN is the author and recipe creator of Peanut Butter and Jilly. Jill was born and raised in the South. She has six siblings, five of whom are boys, and most are picky eaters. She's always loved preparing food for her family, and her food is inspired by the dishes she loved growing up.

Jill began following a plant-based diet several years ago, mostly for health reasons, but also for overall compassion for the planet. She struggled with many of the recipes she found online. Oftentimes, they were complicated, with expensive, obscure and highly processed ingredients. As a nutrition expert and self-proclaimed foodie, Jill sought to create her own recipes that were low-calorie, used whole foods and were simple and easy and absolutely delicious. She began sharing her recipes online, and within a year, Peanut Butter and Jilly had hundreds of thousands of readers and gained national media and press.

Her readers love her simple, healthy, family-friendly vegan recipes. Her goal is to make vegan and gluten-free cooking and baking easy for everyone and inspire more people to live a plant-based lifestyle. She'd like to help others impact their health and the planet, while making room for the sweet and savory treats she is known for. And her number one mission in life is to spread as much cheer as possible!

INDEX